"Wow, I couldn't put it down. It took a great deal of courage to share that background info. The book should be required reading for all high school students."
—ARMANDO F. SANCHEZ, Founder and Executive Director, Latino Scholastic Achievement Corporation

"Daniel Gutierrez has 'stepped into his greatness.' It is evident on each page of his book that through his experiences, and allowing himself to remain humble and grateful, he has found his calling. By sharing his story it allows readers to see aspects of themselves and to learn tools to begin on their own path to greatness. Dan's book is full of lessons and inspiration. I hope many will read this book and benefit from it as I have."
—DR. JULIE L. OSBORN, LCSW, Psy.D.

"This book should be required reading for high school students! The lessons to be learned are invaluable in the effort to achieve your goals."
—SUSIE CASTILLO, Miss USA 2003

"We need more Latino leaders, and *Stepping Into Greatness* is a guide to empower the Latino community. *Stepping Into Greatness* opens your eyes to the possibilities of a better life."
—RENZO DEVIA, Founder, Urban Latino TV and American Latino TV

"Daniel's book provides us with profound insights into the elusive goal of success. I learned that it is not just hard work and tenacity that characterizes success, but it has more to do with how we handle setbacks, failures, and challenges and what lessons we learn from these experiences. Great job."
—RAUL YZAGUIRRE, President, National Council of La Raza

As a new entrepreneur, I was extremely motivated, captivated and entranced as I read each chapter. I didn't want to stop reading. I felt like I was Rocky . . . you get a beating, but you never stop believing or achieving. Life is full of challenges. It's those who are focused, determined and have a vision that will succeed. This book is outstanding, and I highly recommend it to anyone, especially our youth.

—ADDY MAU, Owner, Heaven Sent Jewelry

STEPPING INTO GREATNESS

Success Is Up to YOU!

Daniel Gutierrez

Penmarin Books
Roseville, California

Editorial Offices   *Sales and Customer Service Offices*
Penmarin Books   Midpoint Trade Books
1044 Magnolia Way   27 West 20th Street, Suite 1102
Roseville, CA 95661   New York, NY 10011
(916) 771-5869   (212) 727-0190

Penmarin Books are available at special discounts for bulk
purchases for premiums, sales promotions, or education.
For details, contact the publisher. On your letterhead,
include information regarding the intended use of the
book and how many you wish to purchase.

ISBN: 1-883955-35-1

For information about the Fundraising Through
Empowerment program, contact the publisher
at Penmarin Books' editorial offices.

Cover photo by Starla Fortunato.
Cover design by James Zach.

Printed in the United States of America.

THIS BOOK IS DEDICATED

to my mother,

Catalina Ruiz,

who by her actions taught me to never give up.

And to my son,

Aaron Daniel Gutierrez,

whose existence in my life has given me the courage to wake up every day, and to leave not only a legacy for him, but for our entire world.

Contents

Preface

*We all bond in our brokenness. It is
there in that special place that we find
the similarities and are allowed see the
greatness in each other.*

. . . .

As I look back on my life, "accepting your greatness"
means mainly that you need to take a look at yourself. I
know that most of my life I ran from who I was, and I
wanted to be something I wasn't. I wanted to be taller,
faster, better looking, whiter—everything but me. Accepting your greatness is about understanding that you
are created in the image of greatness, and that is enough.
Accepting your greatness is about looking deep inside
at the hurt and the pain and realizing that a lot of the
things we assume about ourselves just aren't true. I
wasn't a failure, although I had failed many times.

Accepting greatness is also accepting other people's
greatness—for who they are and for what they do. Accepting greatness is about self-love, self-acceptance, self-
realization, and ending the struggle and competition with

yourself. Accepting your greatness means stepping up to realize success.

Accepting my own greatness meant taking a look at all of the rough patches of my life—the relationships, the failed marriages, financial troubles, uncooperative colleagues—and realizing that I was the common denominator. If there was going to be change in my life, it would have to begin with me.

Accepting my greatness meant stepping into the power I have been given in order to succeed at whatever I want to choose, including writing this book. To be honest, I've found the process very uncomfortable. "What's the point?" I kept asking myself. Accepting your greatness is about acting instead of just thinking about it. It's about taking a look at all the successes in life and finding a way to duplicate them, about taking basic principles and making them work.

This book in written in three parts. Part One is my story. It is not written so that you can feel sorry about my past or even are in awe about it. It is written so that you can see that I am human and just like you. It is an opportunity to begin to look for those similarities that allow us to grow. It is not our story that defines us but rather what we do with it.

Part Two is a diary of the period of time when I was creating my dream. It allows you to see what it really took for me to reach it. This is not a self-help book about what you should do but rather what it takes to be successful.

Many times I have been asked what I do to stay focused and motivated. Part Three is just that. These chapters have exercises that will allow you not only to accept your greatness but step into it. I encourage you not only to look at this as a self-help book but to take to heart the stories I've told and find ways to weave the lessons inherent in them into your life. That way, you'll be able to see the greatness in you. Look at the world and find ways to collaborate rather than separating yourself. In a world where it seems that we are most interested in our differences, we should focus on our similarities instead.

This book was written for everyone, regardless of color or ethnicity. I call myself the World's Number One Latino Motivator, but in essence I am a "world motivator" who just happens to be Latino. This book is a guide for the CEO of a major corporation as well as a single mother at home. It applies to all of us, because in our "hurry here, hurry there" world, with all of its positions, tasks, titles, worries, and ambitions, there is one thing that rings true: We are all human. At the moment we close our eyes before going to bed at night, we are all equal. We all agonize just the same over our businesses, children, schools, and finances and the state of our world. In that moment, in that final thought before we succumb to sleep, we are deciding what our world should be. It is in that moment of humanness that we are truly confronted with self-leadership. It's not a question of "what can I do?" but rather "what will I be?"

As you read this book and identify with my story, think of the successes you have had and look for the times you have stepped into your own greatness. Then send me a letter or an e-mail! I would love to read your stories.

I am blessed to have this time with you. As you enter the world of self-leadership, keep in mind that Success Is Up to YOU!

Acknowledgments

It is said that it takes a village to raise a child. It is also true that it takes a village of supporters, mentors, and teachers to write and publish a book.

It would take me an entire decade to thank all the people that have influenced my life and led me to the place I am today. This book has been a labor of love, not just for me, but for all those who, in the process, crossed its path.

There are people in this world who come and go and never make a mark. Then there are those who change the way I see life and add color, allowing me to see everything in a much richer way. Patricia A. S. Hernandez is one of those people. Not only did Patricia skillfully take my thoughts and help bring them to life on the page, she also held my heart gently as I relived some very difficult times in my life. I owe her a great deal of gratitude for her editing, her guidance and her professionalism. Anyone lucky enough to work with her will feel the same way I do.

Hal Lockwood, my publisher at Penmarin Books, is another person who has changed the way I see life. I thank him for his guidance and encouragement in writing and publishing this book, and for his conviction in helping to create "Fundraising Through Empowerment," a cooperative distribution program that allows Penmarin and me to partner in giving profits back to organizations and communities that so desperately need them. It's a level of social responsibility we should all consider.

I want to thank my dear Dr. Sande Herron. Sande has been my friend, my therapist, my pastor, and my mother away from home. Sande gave me the confidence to not only accept my greatness, but to hold a vision for me until I could step into it. Without Sande, this book, and my career as a speaker, would not be possible.

I want to thank Monica Cousins for her dedication in raising our son, Aaron Daniel, and for loving him while giving me the space to write this book and chase my dreams.

Finally, I want to thank all the people who have continued to support me and believe in me by encouraging me to pursue my passion. To all those who have crossed my path and made my life better, you know who you are. I would like to specifically name a few mentors and teachers who, with or without their knowledge, guided me: Moctesuma Esparza, Jim Ort, Joe Conway, Dr. Mark Siegal, Bob Cavindar, Dr. Robert Schuller, Julie Osborn, Renee Perry, Kristie Yeckel, Rick Gilliam, Robert Gordillo, Nancy Vogel, Yasmin Davidds, Rafael Colon, Ken Weller, Dick Schultz, June Davidson, Mike Aguilera, and finally, my entire family back in Texas. Thank you all.

Tell Me Your Story

All around the globe, people just like you are reading this book and stepping into greatness, and I want to hear about your successes. I will incorporate them into a book called *Stories of Greatness*, which will share with the world how ordinary people stepped into extra-ordinary greatness! If you feel you have a story to tell, send it to stories@danielgutierrez.com. You will be notified by e-mail if your story is selected.

I look forward to reading about your greatness.

DANIEL GUTIERREZ

PART ONE

WE ALL HAVE
A STORY,
SO WHAT

Chapter 1

Boy from Midlothian

*Sometimes I wondered if God was somehow
trying to challenge me. It seemed that He was
trying to mold me into a beautiful vase, even
when I would have settled for being an ashtray.*

● ● ● ● ● ● ● ● ● ● ●

My father came home drunk, as he often did, one night
when I was five. It was my younger brother's birthday,
but instead of candles and presents, what I remember
is his one hand around my mother's throat, and the
other brandishing a knife. "I'll kill you, *perra!*" he
screamed at her, while my brother and sister sat silently
shaking on the couch. I felt paralyzed. I stood there like
a statue while my mother screamed for me to call the
police. I couldn't. I didn't know how to use the phone. I
was powerless to help my mother. All I could do was cry
and beg for him to leave her alone. Eventually, alerted
by a neighbor, the police arrived and hauled him off.
That was the last time I saw him alive. Within a year, he
died in a car crash in Florida.

That night, so long ago, would be one of the most
formative events of my young life. I was helpless, and it

terrified me. That night I decided something about myself: I was a failure. Later on, when things got tough, I would check out—I'd quit instead of seeing things through. Truth be told, on my darkest days I can still hear a little voice in the back of my head, and I can clearly imagine myself—a skinny, little, terrified boy— unable to help the woman who cared for me the best way she could. My mother was my life, and I had been useless.

Until a certain age, much of the success I achieved was not born of a desire to win but was the result of a fear of failure. It was that fear that drove me until, slowly but surely, over a long period of experience, trust, and maturity, I came to accept my own greatness as a man, as a Latino, and as a human being. That little voice in the back of my head, the one that said I was no good at anything, the one that sounded like a freight train rushing between my ears, finally began to diminish when I realized that I was created by my god to achieve. I could never get rid of the voice completely, but I sure could mute it and do my utmost to continue onward and upward.

· · · · · · · · · · ·

Reaching your dreams is about having faith
that what you hold true in your heart will
manifest itself with hard work.

· · · · · · · · · · ·

My mother was a migrant worker in Dixon, Califor- nia, so we spent a lot of time out in the fields. We were very poor. She raised the three of us for a long time on welfare and government cheese (a source of mockery now, but something we needed to survive). Sometimes the *queso, frijoles, tortillas,* and *huevos* were all we had to eat for weeks on end. In retrospect, I see that my mother's life must have been terribly difficult, more difficult than my young mind was able to comprehend, and she worked very hard to provide for us, all on her own much of the time. Yet I never, ever heard her complain. She had an amazing ability to endure adversity—something I strive to emulate every day.

Back in the 1960s—about 1968—Dixon was a very small town in the agricultural-based Central Valley. We lived in a shabby, green, two-bedroom house, which my mother kept immaculate. After a day of exhausting manual labor in the hot sun, she would work just as hard when she came home, cooking and cleaning before she was finally able to rest—briefly. She probably slept less than five hours a night, even on weekends. A giant fig tree in the front yard lent some much-needed beauty to the depressed neighborhood where we lived at the edge of town. My brother and sister and I used an abandoned cemetery as a playground. We were close as children, but as adults we would all go our own way in an attempt to escape the memories of our upbringing. As kids, though, we knew we were lucky to have each other because no matter how bad it got, we had each other.

Until the age of six, I didn't speak English very well, and I spoke with a heavy accent, which provoked ridicule in school. I hated being taunted. I loved to smile, though, which often got me in trouble. Aching for attention and the validation I didn't get at home, I'd act up in class, and I'd usually be called out for talking. I've always had a very distinctive and loud voice, so even when I was whispering, I could be heard over the other kids. I remember the principal telling my furious mother that he didn't understand how such a quiet kid could get into so much trouble. At the time, it made me angry to be singled out that way, but later in life that loud, distinctive voice would be recognized as a talent instead of something to be ashamed of. I really just wanted to be liked and validated.

I also sensed that some kids' parents didn't want me around because I wasn't the right color. Even at such a young age, I had a strong tendency to focus on the negative. I was already very cynical; I had a perpetual feeling of not knowing what I was supposed to do, how I was supposed to act, or why I had even been born. Beyond my mother, I had no real role models in my life. I was winging it most of the time, and rules in general made very little sense to me.

On the outside, I was fairly quiet, but on the inside, I was full of roaring turmoil. What overshadowed everything else was my own self-doubt, especially after my mother declared me to be the "man of the house." At the age of seven, she sat me down and declared that she expected me to take a larger role in caring for my siblings. Above all else, I was forbidden to get sick. No one had the time or energy for that. I took my responsibility seriously, although it was crushingly intimidating. All I really wanted was to be a regular kid with a regular family. What I wanted was to go fishing and camping like the sons on TV did with their dads. I wanted someone to love me and care for me. These childhood fantasies would fall woefully short of reality.

When I was ten, my mother moved us from California to Midlothian, Texas, along with a man she'd met—my future stepfather. I was enrolled in a new school in a new state, and I felt like an outsider all the way around. I was never very popular throughout middle school, and my acne limited my interaction with girls. My situation was made more difficult because I was one of only a few Hispanics in school—one of the "Mexicans," they would say with a sneer.

On top of that, I was also the smallest of the boys in my class. For our final physical education exam in eighth grade, we were required to pass a rope-climbing test. I had two choices: I could prove to myself and everyone else that I was capable, or I could allow the voice in my head to ring true. I remember every detail of that day clearly. Most of the boys took around fifteen minutes to climb the rope and ring the bell at the top. There were a couple of guys who had some trouble. As soon as I wrapped my hands around the rope, my knees began to shake. It took me what seemed like two hours to grab the rope, pull myself up with every ounce of my strength, which wasn't formidable, and repeat the motion over and over. Looking up was torture because the bell seemed so far away, but I was actually making progress. When I pushed out the last iota of energy I had and swished my fingertips against the bell, my life changed in a profound way. I had conquered that nagging voice. I had won. I learned that day that I could act in spite of my self-doubt; I could push through fear and frustration and anger and sadness, and I could come out victorious. It just hurt like the dickens, both physically and emotionally.

It was a powerful accomplishment in my eyes, and with a new sense of self-confidence, I decided I wanted to play football in high school. I feared I wasn't big enough or fast enough, though. But being on the football team would help me make friends, I was sure of that, so I spent that summer working out hard, and I got stronger. Now there was a voice encouraging me to counter the other self-defeating voice in my head. This one said, "That's it! It's time to step up to the plate! No more being a victim! Let's see some fight!" It was like a bolt of lightning. I wasn't going to let anyone tell me I was too small or too brown or too poor. As I repeatedly worked my muscles, day in and day out, my body grew both in height and stature, which acted as even more of an incentive. By the start of the school year, I had transformed myself from a weakling to a buffed athlete. I was accepted by the team in my freshman year.

I wasn't done yet, though. The physical goals I'd met brought the realization that hard work could bring results. I had learned that facing something head on rather than running away frequently works, and with my burgeoning confidence, I decided to go out for track. Long-distance running held a special appeal for me. It made me feel strong. The process of pushing on in spite of the agony and of taking another step even though my tank was on empty made me feel empowered like never be-

fore. Passing the finish line, knowing I'd given it everything I had, gave me a feeling of ecstasy. Running long
distances also got me out of the house and gave me
time to think. And for the first time in my life, girls were
noticing me. I loved to win, and I loved the attention
that came with it.

I noticed that speed runners got even more admira-
tion from the coaches and the other kids, so I thought
about entering the 880-yard race at a district track meet.
The coach didn't think I was fast enough, but that didn't
faze me. I asked a friend to borrow his shoes, because
he had the correct type for sprinting. The gun went off
and thirty kids ran like the wind. I focused only on the
ground in front of me, blocking out any distractions,
including the internal ones I still had a tendency to create for myself. The local newspaper ran a photo of me
streaking down the home stretch—the picture made it
look as if I was in the lead, although in the end I placed
sixth. The way I saw it, there were twenty-four other
runners behind me. My coach was shocked. I was honest enough to tell him that the shoes I'd borrowed were
so tight, I'd been racing just to take them off!

When I was twelve, my mom married my new stepfather, Narciso. She seemed to love him, and he seemed
to love her, but I also realized, even at a young age, that
she was in desperate need of companionship and someone to help her with the rigors of daily life. Neither one
of them explained their relationship to us; adult matters were kept private at my house. I resented him terribly, though. First of all, I was ashamed and embarrassed
because he didn't look like any of my friends' dads. We

also argued frequently, and I was furious about him becoming part of my family. He wasn't a kind man—he ranted and raved and told me I was a failure, over and over again. He repeatedly said I'd never amount to anything, that I was "no good." My mother kept her silence in front of him and told me confidentially to just "let it go." He, in turn, resented me because I was another mouth to feed, another distraction for my mother—another responsibility. Things got progressively worse at home, and then I learned that he was involved in drugs and had spent time in jail. It was bad enough being one of the only Hispanic families in town; now I had a shady dude for a stepdad.

Narciso had a relatively good job, and he supported the family to a certain extent, but he had a pronounced dark side that scared all of us. Weird-looking characters came around the house speaking in hushed tones and making exchanges. Sometimes I could tell he was high. I hated him for putting my family in harm's way, and I was afraid that if he went back to jail, my mom would have to go, too. The thought infuriated me, and my rage grew as time went on. I couldn't talk about it because open and honest discussion was not welcome in my home—everything was swept under the carpet— and even my mother acted like nothing out of the ordinary was going on. I thought about turning him in, but I was afraid. His anger intimidated me more than anything else, and I couldn't think of hurting my mother.

Eventually it got so bad that one night, when he was asleep, I crept into his room with a loaded shotgun—his own. While I listened to his guttural snores, I put the muzzle to his head. My finger lingered near the trigger as I sat for what felt like an eternity, thinking about what I was about to do. If I got ten years for my crime, I'd still be in my mid-twenties when I got out. I was actually able to rationalize the act. I looked at my mother and I realized that I would, in effect, be killing her, too. She'd already been through so much. I lowered the weapon and walked away. Within days of that incident, I took my mother's car and drove one hundred miles to my aunt's house in Brownwood, Texas. I was sixteen years old.

I lived with my aunt for a short time, during which I was sued for an accident I was involved in. To my astonishment, the father of a high school friend in Midlothian, Bob Hinds, came to my aid. He was a sheriff and his wife worked for child protective services. Somehow Bob's father got me out of trouble. Bob also told me that I was missed at school, and that really surprised me. What surprised me even more was that Bob's parents invited me to live with them. I moved back to Midlothian and stayed with the Hinds family during my junior year and reestablished contact with my mother.

At some point, it was suggested that Mr. and Mrs. Hinds become my legal guardians. I spoke to my mother about it, unaware of what her reaction would be. I thought she would be relieved, but instead, her grief was immediate and profound. She said, "If they become your parents, you will no longer be my son." I moved back to my mother's home with the knowledge that I would be graduating soon and that I would then be able to leave home as an adult. My stepfather and I succeeded in avoiding each other most of the time. He still had no idea how close I'd come to killing him.

After I moved back in with my mother, a number of illnesses and injuries sidelined me. In my senior year I had knee surgery after a football injury, but at least there was some honor in that. Later that year, after graduation, I was returning from a party when I fell asleep at the wheel and hit a parked Cadillac at 90 miles an hour. The car's hood shattered the windshield and lacerated my face, tearing half of it so badly it lay on my shoulder. Later the doctor told me it had taken more stitches to fix it than I could ever count. At the time of the accident, I thought my time was up as I stood leaning against the empty car I'd hit. A car stopped and a couple of guys piled out. They were so drunk they could hardly speak. A third man inside the car convinced them to leave the scene without helping me. Minutes later another man stopped and called an ambulance. He saved my life.

Just before the accident I had been released from the hospital after suffering a bad bout of pneumonia. Every time I went to the hospital—for the knee injury, the pneumonia, and the accident—I was put in the same hospital room. The nurses said they were going to name it after me. I'm not superstitious, but that gave me pause. Maybe God was testing me, I thought.

After high school, like most kids, I had no idea what I wanted to be or where I wanted to go. I lacked direction. Every summer, my mother had sent us to Bible camp. It was a win-win situation for everyone. She got a break from the kids and we got hot meals. The church folks had always shown me love and attention, something that was scarce in our home, and that's where I had found the acceptance I so desperately craved. I felt like I belonged there. It was the one place I could go where the color of my skin, what I looked like, or where I came from didn't matter. They always welcomed my siblings and me with open arms and a cheerful demeanor. In fact, relatively speaking, they treated us like we were royalty.

With graduation approaching, I decided to plan my future around the church. I became licensed as a Baptist minister at the age of seventeen, and I worked at the Mount Lebanon Baptist Camp as a lifeguard and a preacher, speaking to 1500 kids at a time. I held a football in one hand while I spoke about standing up for Christ and how difficult that could be—how difficult life in general could be. It was thrilling, and it foreshadowed the path I would take later in life. I found that religion gave me hope. It gave me a pure vision of honesty, kindness, and reaching out to each other—helping people in need, listening to them, and trying to be of help somehow. And the feeling was mutual! It may sound corny to some, but the church community filled my heart.

At the same time, I developed a love for art. An art teacher at school, Patty Crane, took a liking to me and saw some promise in my work. She was one of the first people in my life to actually encourage me. Under her wing, I began to entertain thoughts of what I *could* do rather than what I *couldn't* do. I thought it was crazy at first, but she made me repeat a mantra: "I can do it," that came from somewhere deep inside, despite all the obstacles I had faced. A voice in my head began to say, "You know what? Maybe I *can* have whatever I want!

Maybe I deserve love and respect from everyone, not just the people at church!" In fact, Mrs. Crane thought I had enough talent to stick her neck out for me. With her recommendation, I became the first teenager to be awarded a scholarship to the Southwestern Watercolor Society, in Dallas, to study under artists Warren Color and Clay McGough. I attended the course during my senior year.

Of course, given my nature, I soon became frustrated there. In art class, I had worked on ceramics and drawing projects, but I'd never really picked up a brush and painted forms or nature. It was very intimidating to sit in front of a blank sheet of watercolor paper and be expected to perform. I wanted to be as good as my teachers, beginning on day one! I had no idea at the time that in order to be successful, you have to be willing to go through a working process, beginning with the first steps, and build on that, which was literally what the process of creating art was. I wanted to paint the picture immediately, not to take the time to do it. Warren did demonstrations every day, while we students watched him create magic with bright purples, blues, and reds that leapt off the paper and came alive right in front of our eyes. I sometimes found myself envious rather than inspired.

I was very grateful to have received this wonderful opportunity, but I had brought all of my insecurities with me. One afternoon, I sat on the bank of the Guadalupe River and I picked up my brush. I looked at my paper and I said to myself, "Nah, I can't do this." When I told Warren, he said, "Go home, then." I was seventeen years old—fragile and egotistical.

"Go home?" I murmured, as it all sunk in.

"Yeah, go home. We don't deal with negative attitudes here," he answered. I hated him for saying it, but I respected him for caring enough to set me straight. I ended up staying for the full course.

· · · · · · · · · · ·

*Sometimes everything we are
looking for is right inside.*

· · · · · · · · · · ·

My high school graduation had very special meaning for me, as it does for all teenagers on the verge of becoming adults. I had proven things to myself. I was now stronger, both physically and emotionally, and I had my own life, free of family troubles and responsibilities, to look forward to. The icing on the cake was when my classmates voted me the friendliest guy in our senior class. Bob had been right. I hadn't recognized it before, but my peers really liked me. For our graduation ceremony I auditioned to sing "Through the Years," by Kenny Rogers, and was selected for the honor. My mother told someone that she didn't even know I could sing. My yearbook motto was Mrs. Crane's famous "I can do it!"

I enrolled in religious studies at Howard Payne University in Brownwood, Texas, with a scholarship from the church. I was elated about going to college. I finally felt like my life was going in a positive direction, and my future was clearly in the ministry. I was a sober person; I didn't drink or curse; I studied the Bible. I dreamed of buying an RV with a kitchen so I could travel the country teaching the gospel. In retrospect, I'm thankful that I had a strong foundation in the church before I got to college. My faith would be tested in the years to come.

During my freshman year in college, I began to pursue leadership roles, particularly because my peers encouraged me. With my background of speaking to large audiences, I knew how to convey powerful messages about the things I believed in, which at the time were God and the church. I was voted senator of my freshman class, and at the same time, I was voted president of the men's Bible study group at my seventeen-story dormitory building. I was challenging myself intellectually, studying Hebrew and Greek, and I was taking singing lessons.

I also applied for a job as a boxing coach at a juvenile detention center in town. In high school, I had tried my hand in the ring, and I enjoyed everything about it except getting hit. In college it seemed like a good way to make a couple of bucks and to help some young kids in trouble. I was required to undergo intensive psychological testing as part of the interview process. The boys in the detention center were only a few years younger than I was, and the administrators wanted to see if I could handle the pressure. When the results came in, the psychologist pulled me into his office and told me, "Danny, you have a very strong ability to persuade people to follow you. Be careful where you lead them."

I had initially formulated a plan to follow God as a result of what I'd experienced at home. My family had never shown affection. It was almost as if there was a silent code—we were to assume that we were loved, and that we loved back; it just remained unspoken. I also figured, perhaps subconsciously, that if I was following God, I was taking the opposite route my stepfather had. The most important thing for me was that the church and the college provided me with a safe environment. I was under the impression that I could absolutely trust the people around me. Then, in the space of twenty-four hours, I had a catastrophic revelation.

On weekends I traveled to local churches to speak. A Baptist church in Brownwood extended an invitation, which I readily accepted. I never turned down an opportunity to spread the word. The night before I was to deliver my message, though, I went out with a group of young men who were also studying to be ministers. It had always been my understanding that students at Bible school behaved in a certain way: They followed God and acted accordingly. I was naïve. That night I saw a lot of things that I hadn't witnessed since I lived with my stepfather. These men, who were supposedly devoted to the righteous life, drank alcohol, smoked pot, and regaled each other about where they found girls to have sex with. I sat there silent, my eyes agape, wondering how I had jumped from my safe, stable world to this new, dangerous, and disturbing one. I was destroyed. In fact, my sense of loss was so profound it temporarily undermined my trust in God. My reaction was so strong I decided not to preach at the church the next day. Mainly I felt angry. The sense of greatness of purpose and of togetherness in pursuit of good that inspired me to speak disappeared. I lost my faith in people, and I felt at odds with the world. I had put all of my eggs in one basket, and now the bottom of the basket had fallen out. If these men, who claimed to be pure and holy, were so corrupt, then where in the world would I go to find stability? Who could I trust?

I had a profound, extended identity crisis. As if I'd been taken over by another persona, my frame of mind shifted completely. That night I found myself vacillating between staying the course and throwing in the towel. I became more and more resolved to give up on what I had thought was my chosen path. If both sides had fought, it would have been a war, but the voice that had encouraged me and given me positivity in the past vanished, and the dark side took over. I decided to leave Howard Payne and my old life behind and to switch gears immediately.

The next day when I returned to college, the first thing I did was to go to a liquor store and buy myself a beer—a tall boy. I went and sat in my convertible and looked at the can. A beautiful woman pulled up beside me. She looked at me and apparently sensed that there was something very wrong. She turned and said, "Hey, please don't do it. Don't give in." But another voice spoke louder: my old personal interior critic. Maybe I had been a "goody two shoes" long enough. Maybe I had been missing out on all the fun. Maybe I didn't need to take life so seriously. Maybe it was time for me to go out into the real world and do what everyone else did, thereby denying what I'd always assumed was right for me. I turned away from her, reached down, cracked that beer open, and drank it in one gulp. Chemical confidence was soon to replace the security of faith.

Chapter 2

You Can Run, But
You Can't Hide

*You can chase your heart, or you can
give in to that insidious voice in
your head that tells you, "I can't!"*

• • • • • • • • • • •

That beer I swallowed in the liquor store parking lot was
the first of many, and my life would take a polar change
in the years to follow. There was no question, I wouldn't
stay at Howard Payne University. I decided to leave HPU
because I had lost faith in the idea of "following God" as
a career. At that point, I simply didn't want anything to
do with God at all. I turned my back. Until then, I had
been a church-going, God-fearing, non-drinking, non-
dating, boring guy. Now I was set on having fun. It
wouldn't be until much later that I would learn the truth
about spirituality and my own personal relationship with
God. For now, I wanted to experience the things I'd previously rejected. I dropped out and enrolled at North
Texas State University in Denton. And like a kid in a

candy store without any rules, I went hog wild. In hindsight, I know that the thing I was still desperately searching for was validation, however it came. I still had no idea that validation comes from within.

I decided on NTSU because they had the best art department in the state. That would be my new focus, and it brought with it different people, different places, and different situations. I was exposed to an entirely new world. Where I had formerly been surrounded with what I thought was morality and stability at HPU, I was suddenly surrounded by temptation. I was a healthy young man, and I appreciated healthy young women very much. For the first time, I was exposed to parties, fraternities, sororities, beer by the keg, cigarettes, drugs, and a general attitude of "We're young, we're indestructible, and we're going to rage all night, every night!" Terry Cooper, a high school classmate, became my roommate. He introduced me to cool people, hip hangouts, and cocaine. The first time I saw Terry surrounded by pretty girls snorting lines of powder off a coffee table, I resisted. But it wasn't long before my curiosity was piqued, and with something as insidious as coke, the first time is never the last.

Soon it became a way of life; I was drinking alcohol and snorting coke pretty much on a daily basis. I liked the way it made me feel. It gave me an all-powerful confidence, it made me feel happy, and it gave me the ability to socialize with the big men on campus—and their girlfriends. In the beginning, it never occurred to me that it was all false. My body was still young and strong enough to weather the wear and tear. Drugs are so pow-

erful, particularly coke, and I got into a morass of denial. I actively pushed guilt, fear, my stepfather, and my
own safety to the very farthest recesses of my mind.
Emotions and thoughts that bummed me out I tossed
away like so much garbage. Even Terry questioned my
prolific drug use and moved out. As the saying goes, I
went to a party, but I didn't come back for months.

On the surface, everything seemed to be working out
for me, which gave justification to my vices. Everyone
has a gift, and I had been blessed with a personality
that drew people to me. Although I'd been a shy and
awkward kid, tormented by terrible incidents and voices,
I had always been easy with a smile. People had gone
out of their way for me on numerous occasions. I recognized this characteristic as a powerful one by the time I
got to college. It was up to me to decide how I was going
to use it. I used my personality to charm my way into
getting just about anything I wanted, be it girls, drugs,
favors, or opportunities. I also had passion. I've always
had a fire inside me, and it burns hot sometimes. When
something interests me, I put everything I have into it
with the force of an erupting volcano.

Something I lacked, however, was community identity. From the time I entered kindergarten, I never made
any association with my roots. Was I American? Was I
Latino? Did I care? I had grown up in a predominantly
White town, and I'd had very little exposure to Mexican
culture and people. Like many Mexican Americans, especially at the time, I assimilated to the surrounding
culture. I wanted to fit in with everyone else. I was at-
tending a mainly White school, and the Mexican-Ameri-

can organization on campus encouraged me to run for a leadership position in their group. I simply didn't respond to them. I had no real understanding of what my role would be, what I would be standing for. And I wasn't, at the time, interested in learning.

Instead, I began thinking outside of the box. When the opportunity came to run for office for the Young Republicans of North Texas, I jumped at it. I joined the group more out of rebellion than anything. Part of my newfound philosophy was to do the opposite of anything that was expected of me. Obviously it would have made sense, both personally and professionally, to support the Latino organizations on campus. But I enjoyed being controversial. It got me more attention. As soon as I was told that it would be a crazy idea to run for president, going totally against the grain, I put on a campaign and won the election by a landslide. It was a fantastic learning experience—one of the few positive things I took part in during a time when I was literally destroying my body with drugs. A highlight was my debate with Dick Armey, who would go on to become an influential congressman. I knew at that point that I did not specifically want to be a politician, but I did see a future in leadership of some kind. I had enough foresight to understand that what I was learning there would be paramount to my future. I paid attention.

At the same time, I was elected president of my fraternity pledge class, Delta Sigma Pi. It was such an honor to hold these offices. It was a heady thing. I spent a lot of time digesting the fact that people responded to me so well, but I struggled with the idea that I could get elected to a position like this and still feel insecure. Little by little, though, I was beginning to lose some of that terrible cynicism and defeatism. I'm sure many people wouldn't have believed me if I told them how I really felt about myself. I was living a paradox. On the one side, I was a successful, energetic, charismatic young man; on the other, I was still a little boy, lost in a nightmare, on the verge of smashing anything good that came my way.

My coursework was going very well. I had some talent as an artist, and I truly loved what I was doing. The idea of "creating" always appealed to me, although I knew that artists didn't make any money. Then again, I didn't know at the time that if you do what you love, everything else follows. I was studying interior design and industrial technology, primarily because there were a lot of cute girls in the program, but also because I wasn't sure which field to concentrate on. In my mind, I just wanted to be an artist.

Again I was impatient. I enjoyed my time in the classroom, but I wanted to be out in the world, making things happen. Most of my peers and teachers told me I wouldn't get a job because I didn't have any experience, or even a portfolio. I was determined, though, so I grabbed the Yellow Pages and started dialing and working my personality. I called dozens of interior design firms until I happened upon a woman who, after an earful of my charming banter, hired me right on the phone. The firm specialized in carpet, drape, and furniture treatments, and during that first conversation, she told me that she had a rather difficult job she needed done: the repair of an octagonal glass-top table with an Egyptian motif worth seven thousand dollars.

"Do you think you can do it?" she asked.

Without a second's hesitation, I answered, "Sure!"

I admittedly had a hard time saying no to anything. She offered me $100 an hour to do the work. I had my first big job.

In truth, I had no idea how to reproduce images on glass. I didn't even know which kind of paint to use. It was the Christmas holiday, but I didn't go home; the job had to be done by January 1st. I agonized over it. It was extremely complex, and I was a novice, albeit a determined one. I took my time and worked meticulously, often with great frustration. I was terrified about each aspect of the process. When I eventually worked up the courage to remove the tape from the final product, I felt elated. The table had come out beautifully—a triumph. It was my greatest accomplishment yet. When my client came to pick up the table, she praised my work and later boasted about my talent to her colleagues and customers. I knew that I'd made her look good. I had created a work of art to be proud of, even though I'd begun without a clue as to how to proceed. I remembered Mrs. Crane in high school saying, "You can do it, Dan." Yes, I could do it.

I also began to pick up on "walking the walk," so to speak. If I was going to take my place in the world, I was going to have to learn to present myself like a man of importance. I had learned that people take you as seriously as you deserve to be taken. I knew that in most cases, if I could get some face time with someone, I could convince them of anything.

The first step was to have the gumption to take the first step. Mr. Trammell Crowe was a world-renowned developer and someone I wanted to do business with. I had read about him in the newspapers and in *Architectural Digest* and knew that just about every building in Dallas had his name on it.

When the interior design firm I was working for was hired to do a job in his multimillion-dollar home, the experience of just seeing the place left a lasting impression on me. In the neighborhood where I lived, there were torn-up screen doors on many houses. At Crowe's house, it took two people just to open the front door. Each room represented a different part of the world, and the solarium had once belonged to the Queen of England. Crowe had had it dismantled, transported by ship, and rebuilt on his property. He then constructed the house around it.

One day Mr. Crowe was at the house at the same time I was, and he introduced himself and shook hands with me. The fact that he even talked to me, the hired help, was amazing. I saw myself pretty small compared to this large icon.

But that was also the day I decided to make the best of a potential opportunity. I looked up his office address, put on my best suit, walked into his building with authority and declared, "I have an appointment with Trammell Crowe."

"You're not in the book," the receptionist said.

"That must be wrong," I said, holding up my briefcase as if it contained stacks of hundred dollar bills. "It's very important that I see him, very important."

She let me through, and I took the elevator to his private office and paraded through the grandiose foyer as if I belonged there. I was nearly breathless at the sight of the most beautifully furnished office I'd ever seen, especially drawn to the models of the buildings this man was going to erect elegantly displayed in lit glass cases. All I had to do now to see Mr. Crowe was to get past his private secretary.

"Young man, go home," she said, without even looking up.

All I could do was laugh on the way home. I knew I was defeated, but I took it in stride. I had shown some gumption.

· · · · · · · · · · ·

Sometimes being stuck provides the impetus
to look up and find solutions outside.

· · · · · · · · · · ·

Living away from home and in a college environment, working, throwing myself behind organizations, and simply maturing had helped me develop my own unique personality—one I accepted. I'd always felt a need to fit in, but that was shifting. I did a lot of thinking about personal power, although I remained humble. I still used coke, however, and I was still using my power in the wrong ways. I even began taking drugs with my stepfather. In this aspect, I embodied everything I'd vowed not to be, but the coke kept pulling me back, as if I had no will of my own. I was experiencing a struggle between good and bad. The good thing was, now I knew what I was doing was bad. Now the denial was gone, and it was replaced by a feeling of guilt and fear. I knew what was right and wrong; I knew better.

For the first time, I saw clearly that the dark side of me was fed whenever I gave into the temptation to do cocaine and that the things that orbit the drug scene— women, false adoration, and being high—were thrilling, but they were dangerous and elusive as well. When a boy makes the decision to get involved in drugs, I can, to this day, sympathize. The lure of money, power, and sex can be overwhelming. The honest truth is that pleasurable things can result from evil roots.

When it came to women, there were plenty around when I was using coke. I had some cash and some nice clothes. I could be charming and fun to be around. But one girl in particular, Julie, mesmerized me from day one. She was only seventeen; I was twenty-two. The first time I asked her out, she said no, so I gave chase, which was something I wasn't used to doing. I was dating more women at the same time during that year than I would end up dating for the rest of my life. But within a few months, Julie and I started living together. Julie was the first girl I ever really loved. In 1989, we got married.

For me, being in a relationship, being able to share your life with someone, having someone to love, was what I had always wanted. I had seen terrible abuse between my mother and my father, and I'd vowed never to make that mistake. But I had no idea of what comprised a *good* relationship. I had nothing to base my actions or my words on, and I didn't always trust my gut instinct. My relationship with Julie was abusive, both verbally and emotionally, no matter how hard we both tried. I now know that we were simply too immature to lift each other up rather than tear each other apart. The love we shared was so foreign to me that I sabotaged it, and we divorced before our second anniversary. I felt like a complete failure. Again, I had tried to do something positive and I had ruined everything. Julie picked up and left. She had no choice.

With my self-esteem lower than ever, I belly-flopped. Just as I had given up on my faith the night before I was to speak at the Baptist church, I gave up on personal relationships in general, whether they were business, school, or socially related. I had a problem with generalizing things, I was a perfectionist, and I was very hard on myself.

If I painted one picture I wasn't happy with, I was a failure as an artist; if I had a bad experience with one group of people, then all people were flawed; if I had a troubled relationship with one woman, I'd never have any relationship with anyone at all, ever. The negative voice came back screaming. I was not great. I was not a leader. I was a failure. I was completely overwhelmed by the notion that everything I had believed as a kid was true. I couldn't seem to forgive myself. My marriage had only lasted a year, I had failed as a minister, I had dropped out of school, I had failed at home with my mother and stepfather, I had abandoned my siblings, I used drugs, and as a result of what I was about to do, I would lose my positions with the Young Republicans and my fraternity pledge class.

In 1991, our divorce was finalized. I felt broken and lost, living in an apartment in Dallas with no furniture. One morning, after I'd partied pretty hard the night before, I woke up and grabbed the funny papers. Ziggy was my favorite—I identified with him. As usual, I was amazed by the wisdom a silly comic strip could convey. Alone, broke, scared, and hung over, I laughed out loud for the first time in weeks. Ziggy was looking at a billboard with a great big X on it. "You are right here," the caption read, "and you have no one to blame but yourself." It hit me right in the heart, and I allowed myself some introspection, something I'd been avoiding through booze and denial. I took a good hard look at myself, and I did not like what I saw. What was I going to do? First, I had to fix myself—I was damaged goods.

One of my professors had once told me, "You can run, but you can't hide." When I look back today, he was right. I had spent my life running. I had run from God, I had run from people, and I was continually running from myself. In my heart, I was still the little boy who didn't know how to pick up the phone to save his mother's life. I was an utter failure, and this was manifested in the fact that I sabotaged every opportunity that came my way. I did not trust, love, praise, or accept promises from anyone. I had always wanted to be the best-liked man in the room, but now I was totally alone. I found it hard to believe that people had at one time called me a man of prayer.

I had worked hard to earn one hundred hours of credit at school, but in my junior year, I could no longer afford tuition and supplies, despite the fact that I was spending more time working than studying. I wanted to finish school—I would have been the first in my family to do so—but with no support system, no money, and no ideas, I dropped out of NTSU. Had I known that there were myriad grants and scholarships for Latinos, things might have been different. Because I didn't embrace my heritage, I never even explored such avenues. It simply didn't occur to me.

Something inside of me still wanted desperately to succeed, but it came from a fear of failure, not because I had accepted any of my greatness. I feared being poor; I feared unemployment; I feared missing out on opportunities. I didn't have any life tools yet—I didn't know how to step into my own accomplishments. As I'd done before, I returned to denying the talents I had been blessed with.

The only thing I had ever really succeeded at was the work I'd done, so I decided to focus all of my energy on that. Having tasted some professional success, I was hungry for more, particularly the kind that came with money. A fellow who lived across the street from me was a jeweler. After a number of casual conversations with him, I thought maybe I'd give the diamond business a try. As a kid, I'd always been enthralled by stones (and snakes, which I dissected and put in formaldehyde, to my mother's horror). I didn't see any reason why I couldn't open up a little business of my own, selling gold jewelry, while learning more about diamonds. I leapt into my new career with all the vigor I could muster and with Ziggy's words in mind, and before long I was doing very well, although I didn't have a storefront.

The most fortuitous outcome of this was that I began to distance myself from drugs. I was too busy, I had to wake up and make things happen, I had to present myself properly. Whereas I'd seen friends and acquaintances lose everything because of their drug use, I was turning in the other direction. It was now becoming very clear to me that drugs were costing me money, time, and energy. My use of cocaine diminished. I look back at that fact as something of a miracle. It wasn't so much a matter of willpower as a loss of interest, although I still enjoyed drinking with my college friends. Instead of getting sucked into the abyss of drugs, I focused my energy on business and educating myself.

It wasn't long before I began selling diamonds privately. It wasn't easy to break into the business, and sometimes I had to resort to creative means to get where I needed to go. I didn't have any money, and I had to build relationships in order to succeed. Networking was crucial for success. I got word of some potentially helpful gentlemen in the diamond business who had offices in the World Trade Center in Dallas. Making an appointment by phone was impossible—I was a beginner with no credentials, and they had no time for me. As I had done before, I thought outside of the box. When the mountain won't come to Muhammed, Muhammed goes to the mountain. I knew if I could see the men in person, I could work some magic. I walked into the lobby the same way I'd walked into Trammel Crowe's lobby—as if I belonged—and approached the guard. In a fake Middle Eastern accent, and with a hatful of confidence, I explained that I had an appointment on the twenty-fourth floor. The guard bought my act, and more importantly, the diamond dealers found reason to trust me. Before long, I was signing out tens of thousands of dollars in diamonds to sell.

I knew a guy who had many friends playing for the

Dallas Cowboys. He was generous enough to introduce me to some of the team members, and I began to sell to them privately. At one point, I hosted a party at a private home with a million dollars' worth of jewelry, so the players could shop without being mobbed by fans. When it came down to it, I found that I could always use my personality to make things happen—not in a manipulative manner, but by exuding confidence and determination.

It wasn't long before my dreams were halted by the realities of free-market enterprise, though. Soon after my business began to take off, so did the markets. Both gold and diamonds skyrocketed in demand, and a little guy like me couldn't possibly compete with the big chains on pricing. My business plummeted, and I realized the need to join my competition. I realized the need for more structure in my life, and I thought a steady job would take me in the right direction. I went to work for a chain of jewelry stores—Barry's—and I became one of their top producers.

I started as a simple salesman, but before long they promoted me to management. In all honesty, as a manager I was a tyrant. Working for me was very difficult because I was obsessed with results, not human-to-human communication. I yelled, I threw papers, I had no control, yet I was always able to raise the bottom line. In hindsight, I realize I was managing people the way I saw it done on TV. Bosses on TV usually played up the drama. I don't like to admit it now, but wielding power over people, no matter the means, made me feel good. Perversely, it was a method for me to release all of the pent-up anger and frustration I had harbored inside for so many years.

Barry's gave me the worst store in the district—one they were preparing to close down. I convinced them that I could turn it around. Lo and behold, within a year, my team and I transformed it into the number one store in the district. We were making so much money, the owners allowed me free reign to redesign the store, which was in a predominantly black neighborhood in a mall in south Dallas. The crime rate was high, and during the Christmas holidays the police were forced to open a temporary station in the mall's lobby. There were cops on the roof, in the parking lot on horseback, and in helicopters circling overhead.

I was concerned with building relationships with my clientele, so I treated them as I would the residents of Beverly Hills. On Christmas Eve, one of my best customers came in. He always paid cash. I had an idea of where his money came from, but I didn't care. As far as I was concerned, he was welcome to purchase whatever he wanted, whenever he wanted, however he wanted. The store was packed that night as I showed him a series of diamond rings worth five to ten thousand dollars. Suddenly, he stood up and a semiautomatic pistol fell out of his jacket onto the floor. Everyone froze, but I kept my cool. "Bob," I said, "pick up your gun and get out of here. I don't want to call the police." He sheepishly honored my request and took off. My managers and the other customers were stunned but grateful that I'd kept my cool and turned down the business rather than jeopardize their safety.

A salesman from Chicago used to come by the store in a chauffer-driven limousine to sell us diamonds. I admired him for what he had and what he represented. During one trip he asked me to dinner. I believe the bill for the two of us was over two hundred dollars. I was mightily impressed. Before he dropped me off that night, I asked him a question: "How do I get what you have?"

He laughed out loud. "Son, I like your style. But don't expect anything until you're at least in your late thirties or forties." That wasn't what I wanted to hear.

Despite the store's success, my inner turmoil continued unabated. In a strange way, my ability to sell and manage people almost fueled my fury. I was Napoleonic, but I got results. Then the unthinkable occurred: I found out I was dispensable. I had been thinking all along that there was no way, after the results I had created for the company, that they would ever show me the door. But one day, almost out of the blue, my boss came by the store and fired me. It was an issue of economics, he tried to explain. What I assume that meant was that I had reached a salary ceiling, and they knew someone else could take over my newly successful store for a lot less. I was beyond furious. Was there no one to trust in any situation?

In the end, it was a blessing in disguise. I was forced to explore other paths. I didn't understand then that I needed to live through experiences, both good and bad, to learn all the lessons that life had to offer. I had to learn to prove to myself that if I wanted something badly enough, I would have to weather the storms of life. I would have to do all of my homework and enter into all situations with eyes wide open. That's when I would be worthy of success. My teens had been difficult, and my twenties hadn't proven much easier. I had, however, come out of both periods older, smarter, and wiser, although still liable to commit self-sabotage.

Chapter 3

Fake It 'Til You Make It

*Success is born when our ability to focus
on our dreams is greater than our fixation
on our current problems.*

• • • • • • • • • •

I floundered for a while, and then I set out to find a new job. A couple of brothers I knew were in the cellular phone business, and I decided to come on board. We had a small office in North Dallas, and we focused mainly on switching customers from their own carrier to one we represented. After some brainstorming, I came up with the idea of selling accessories. In the early '90s, cell phones were still new to the market, and accessories were the way to make money. The brothers made me an official partner.

In my view, focusing on the international market seemed like the way to go. I soon learned that we could buy battery eliminators for pennies compared to what most folks were paying retail. There were very high margins—up to 400 percent—to be made by doing business with foreign countries. I let my confident side take over in almost a robotic way, and I called the consulates of several countries, mainly in South America. I pitched my idea as if it were the greatest thing since sliced bread. Soon I was in business with a group of Australians who were paying $50 to $100 for these battery eliminators. I could save them almost 50 percent and still make good money.

The Costa Rican consulate included us in their request for an estimate in a multi-million-dollar cellular buy, and I was thunderstruck to come out the victor. But I never filled the order. In fact, I never even called them back. The plain truth was, I had gotten way too far ahead of myself. Here was a platinum opportunity, but, as usual, I got scared. I had no idea how to fill such a large order, and I had never expected them to respond to my initial inquiry, let alone ask me to bid on the cell phone deal. I had been trying to think outside the box, again, and I had been successful. I just couldn't seem to keep up the momentum of success. Instead I froze up like the proverbial deer in the headlights. I didn't have any appreciation for the notion that success came with a progression of small steps. At the time, for me, it was easy money: easy come, easy go.

Especially in the aftermath of my divorce, I had been looking for validation from outside. It was a recipe for disappointment. I could never control other people's thoughts or actions, and I was feeling more mistrustful of people in general than I ever had before. The kind of people I was attracting weren't the kind of people I wanted to do business with. If I wanted successful people around me, there were some things I needed to learn first.

What I really needed was a business that would be around for more than a year. It was time to step back and reanalyze my career strategy. I needed structure—something I hadn't learned at college, especially as an art major. During the time I'd been there, the stability of working for an established company like Barry's had been a source of comfort, although they had simply kicked me out when they'd seen fit to do so, like the brothers I'd worked for. I craved something reliable—something structured. I wanted to know how a real business worked, from the minute the doors opened until they were locked up at night. I wanted to learn how bills were paid and how profits were made. I had God-given talent, but I lacked basic Business 101 skills. I had to observe; I had to listen. I decided to look for a very traditional job, even if I had to start at an entry-level position. After having made a lot of money in speculative businesses, six bucks an hour would be very humbling. It was the best thing that ever happened to me.

After a short search, I took a part-time job at Best Buy electronics as a car speaker and radio salesman. I didn't know anything about electronics. On my first day, my boss asked me, "What do you know?"

"Nothing," I said. I may not have known much about the product, but I did know how to work a customer—how to figure out what they really wanted. I've found that most people just want validation; they want reassurance that what they think they believe is true. I relied on my awareness and personality, and I listened to the client. I became a master of the old saying, "Fake it 'til you make it." I've heard that a man's level of intelligence is not measured by how much he knows but by whether he knows how to look up the answer. If I really needed to, I'd just go and get a product manual and read right out of that!

Slowly but surely, things began to take off for me. Within a few months of starting at Best Buy, I decided to quit drinking and focus on pulling myself together. No one told me to stop; I just was tired of the rollercoaster I'd been on since I'd left the ministry. When I decided to quit doing cocaine, I awoke one morning and went cold turkey. The result was a week of awful days. I perspired and trembled, wrapped up in sweat-soaked sheets, wondering if it would ever end. On the third day of detox, the dealer I'd been buying from came around to drum up business. I told him I had quit and had no need for it. It was one of the hardest things I'd ever done, but still, deep inside, there was a pure, sweet voice telling me to be strong. He said, "Dude! You can't just quit! Ya gotta go to a rehab or something. If you can do this, then you should write a friggin' book!" I just laughed. Now I wanted to prove that I could quit drinking, too, just like that. This was a last-ditch effort to find out why I'd been placed on this earth, what my purpose was in life, what my true passion was. I was never going to find out if I continued to use the crutches of escapism.

Best Buy gave me the opportunity to grow, and I was promoted seven times in a brief period—first to department head, and then to assistant manager of that particular store. I received full benefits, and I felt as if this was the first job I'd had that was really paying me something back for my hard work. My reaction was to work even harder, and I made an effort to learn more about different management styles. I had managed people before, but I had never learned how to get employees to follow willingly—it had always been through threats and discipline. I wanted to learn how to do it the right way. Around that time, a friend said to me, "If you think you're a leader and no one is following, you're just on a very long walk!" People confuse management and leadership. I was leading, but I was not in leadership. I was not managing, either. I was shooting from the hip. To me, management was all about getting people to follow processes. Leadership is about getting people to follow you by example.

The company soon recognized my efforts to learn to lead people both effectively and correctly. My general manager told me I had a lot of talent, and he wanted to "harness" that and get me promoted. Best Buy was going through some growing pains at the time and hadn't yet expanded farther than Texas; but they had faith in people who created results. They had faith in me. It was the first time I had held such a high degree of responsibility, and although I was still torn up inside, I was beginning to heal again. I was learning how to be better than what I was.

In 1994, I got a new assignment. I would be moving to El Paso to act as assistant manager of a store they had newly opened there. I had never traveled on business before, and I felt very important—like I was on a mission. I didn't know much about El Paso, but it would prove to be an enlightening experience. The most important thing I learned was the dynamics of how to succeed by moving forward, and how to explain that concept to my employees. The toughest thing in life is to move forward when it seems like you are failing at everything you touch. Power comes with holding true to what you want until it becomes a reality. I had learned from my mother that no matter how tough things got, it was unacceptable to complain or to give up. I had been forced by circumstances to keep showing up and to keep moving forward, and that's what I tried to instill in my employees. Still, I was pretty green at twenty-eight.

Six months after the store opened, Best Buy offered me the general management position. "Boy, I'm good," I thought. I earned $28,000 a year, the most I had ever made. I had also begun to accumulate stock options. The responsibility of the position was huge, but at the same time, I felt a bit like royalty, both for my personal success and for understanding and getting the most from the people who worked in and shopped at the store. I was a good salesman and even better networker, so I decided to go after the local Hispanic market. At first, I saw my new involvement with Latinos as an opportunity to get them into the store, spending their money. But I also knew that, as part of their marketing plan, Best Buy had an interest in helping the community, and they gave generously. The repercussions of this marketing campaign would have a profound and lasting effect on me.

Networking to the Latino community was a new concept for me, not just from a business perspective, but from a personal perspective, too. Until I moved to El

Paso, my view of myself in terms of ethnicity was very cloudy. I had not exposed myself to the Latino culture, to my roots, even including the way I pronounced my own name. I had always said it with a with an Anglo-Texan accent. In the following months, I corrected myself and pronounced my surname the way it was intended. I went so far as to change my name from Gutierres to Gutierrez, the spelling my ancestors had used. The more exposure I had to my Latino heritage, the more I began to feel as if I belonged. I was eager to learn more about my culture and, by extension, about myself. Later on, one of the things I missed most about El Paso, besides the great food, was driving the short distance across the border to Juarez, Mexico, and enjoying the mariachis in the Plaza Mayor. I felt sincerely connected to something, and I grew proud of my natural roots.

I was given reason to doubt myself once again, however, when the art teacher I'd had during my freshman year at NTSU came into the store. "Oh, I remember you," he said. He remembered me because I had been a loud mouth in his class, but he'd also commented on my artistic talent back then. "What are you doing here?" he asked. "I'm the general manager of the store," I said with pride and a big grin. He shook his head and said, "All that talent. You were so gifted. Remember Rebecca? She's working in Los Angeles for a big art firm." He turned on his heel and left. I was floored. "My gosh," I thought, "did I give up too soon?" His comment lingered with me for a long time.

• • • • • • • • • • •

Life can be so confusing we sometimes
forget to look outside ourselves for answers.

• • • • • • • • • • •

By the spring of 1995, I had spent a long year opening the store in El Paso. Now it was time to stop and reward myself for my hard work. I had always dreamed of going to Europe. I wanted to see the great museums, the pieces of art I had studied in college—I wanted to see the world. I took off with a friend and no itinerary, and as the plane taxied down the runway at Charles de Gaulle Airport in Paris, I was still up in the clouds.

Here I was, a small-town boy who had struggled to make it, fulfilling a dream I never imagined would actually happen. Standing on top of the Eiffel Tower, with Notre Dame, Sacre Coeur, the Louvre, and the River Seine in view, I shook my head and smiled. There were no words to describe the elation I felt. We explored and enjoyed the beautiful French countryside, the vibrant people, the incredible food, and the rich culture. I noticed a difference in the attitude toward drinking alcohol in Europe, which resonated with me. The goal was not to get high but to enjoy the taste and aroma of a good wine with a wonderful meal. Excess was not part of the equation.

In Italy, the art I had only seen in books was more glorious than I had ever thought possible. For me, it was a moving experience to gaze upon Michaelangelo's Pieta in St. Peter's Cathedral, and his statue of David was truly awe inspiring. I had read *The Agony and the*

Ecstasy by Irving Stone, which made me appreciate even more Michaelangelo's genius in the Sistine Chapel. I knew that he had struggled to be a sculptor and painter when his family had insisted that he go into the family business. It hit me that struggle was universal. I had struggled in my life, but so had many great men and women before me—and alongside me.

Venice took my breath away, and as I stood in the Piazza di San Marco, the significance of cultural diversity hit me like a lightning bolt. I had grown up trying to homogenize myself, but I suddenly appreciated people's differences, broadening my horizon. I hadn't been exposed to different cultures, never having left Texas. Our town had more cows than people. Anything I'd experienced about the world had been through books, magazines, or the television. I realized how easy it was to become close-minded and to miss out on the knowledge, viewpoints, and cultural richness that different kinds of people had to offer.

Even though I'd left Texas to see the larger world, I still took some of Texas with me. I brought not one but three sets of cowboy boots with me. You could say I stood out on the beaches of the French Riviera. But in Europe, I learned that being different was actually a blessing. I recognized that I should have been celebrating the similarities in people rather the differences. I realized that variety was truly the spice of life. I wasn't just okay with being Mexican American, I was ready to hold my head up high.

On the train from Nice to Pisa, Italy, I saw a young Italian boy who was going to visit his grandmother. He was visibly excited, jabbering away to his friends and family. His clothes were worn and he was very thin, but he was happier than the richest boy in all of Europe. It was a reminder of how far I'd come. I'd been just like him once, and now I was halfway around the world, experiencing something that had once seemed impossible, realizing truths that would guide my future, both personally and professionally.

I brought back a souvenir from my trip: a different perspective. Back at home, I felt like my life was really beginning to turn around. My struggles weren't over by a long shot, but I was finally conquering what had been terrible self-doubt and a long history of self-sabotage. My trip abroad had rejuvenated me, and I went back to work with a new sense of determination to go beyond what was expected, both from others and from myself. Although I'd always been a go-getter, I raised the bar for myself with the knowledge that both agony and ecstasy were essential aspects of true success.

· · · · · · · · · · ·

My first project when I got back to work was to explore what the ramifications of the North American Free Trade Agreement (NAFTA) were for a business like Best Buy. No one directed me to do this research, but my thinking had been expanded by my travels. Texas was big, but what if we could figure out a way to give credit to Mexican nationals and border town citizens? Mexicans, I learned, were some of the only people who were able to get credit anywhere in the world; they were eligible to receive international credit cards.

I also learned that my limited experience of visiting just the border towns had been misleading. In reality, Mexico not only boasted rich citizens but wealthy cities as well. My vision was to convince a bank to issue Best Buy credit cards, so that Mexicans could cross the border into the United States and purchase whatever they wanted. They certainly had money to spend. If I could get that kind of business, I would at least quadruple my profits. I began networking with people in Mexico to make it happen.

At this point in my career, I had learned to use the leverage that my position at Best Buy carried to create win-win situations which would benefit the customer and give me recognition and praise. Now I began to devise creative ways to use Best Buy's power to gain influence with the media both locally and in Mexico. This increased the visibility of the store, and it gave the Mexican people the impression that we valued their business. I became friendly with the editor of *Diario de Juarez* after developing a healthy respect for the newspaper. After a few preliminary negotiations, I had some very exciting news for the doubters at Best Buy. I called my boss and told him straight up: "Pack a bag. A private plane will be picking us up at 9:30 tomorrow morning. We've been invited to dinner in Chihuahua."

"You're nuts," he said. I don't think he really believed it until he saw the jet waiting for us on the tarmac. "How did you make this happen?" he asked in amazement as we sat being served champagne in plush leather seats. The editor, who was based in Chihuahua, wanted to show us his main plant; he wanted us to see how sophisticated his operation was and how a partnership would benefit all of us. As soon as we arrived, a limousine met us and whisked us away like movie stars to see the city. I had no idea how beautiful Mexico was. Later on that night, we went to the best restaurant in town to be wined and dined. All the while, my boss was beside himself wondering how I had been able to make this happen. And I began to see what I was capable of. I felt very comfortable in the role. I wanted more of this world of big business.

Corporate was still skeptical, but I had big dreams that would not be quashed. I had an undeniable knack for networking. I found that I was able to get what I wanted, specifically by finding out what people *needed*. When I filled that need, my clients would in turn help me. It didn't hurt that I was the general manager of an 18-million-dollar business. I had the ability to suggest where corporate ought to spend their money.

One day a gentleman from one of Mexico's leading banking institutions came into the store to purchase computers. When I learned who he was, I quickly involved myself in the sale. I wanted to get to know him— he was a potential key player in my financing mission. He ended up buying over $36,000 worth of merchandise. I kept in contact with him, and we soon became friends. I explained my vision to him—that Best Buy stores would be built in all the border cities in Texas and Mexico—and he suggested a meeting, offering to fly me and my boss, the district manager in Dallas, to Mexico City. Again, my boss was dubious, but a short time later we were on a first-class flight. If I was to be an integral part of this process, I fully expected to be promoted to manager of these stores when the time came.

Part of my job during that trip was to act as a translator. My Spanish was fairly limited, but I did the best I could. I was honestly so stunned to be there in the first place, I froze up at first. And then I took the leap. I stepped into my greatness. I made a conscious effort to form a mental image of myself as powerful, smart, and strong. On the way back home, my boss looked at me with new eyes. It crushed me at first when the deal didn't go through. Mexico went into a severe recession, and the bank went out of business. But the lesson couldn't be taken back. The experience was ingrained in my mind, and I had to admit to myself that I had achieved something very important. Even more importantly, I had seen—actually witnessed—the world of successful businesspeople, and I knew I could be a part of it. I knew I belonged.

If I had continued to drink to excess or use drugs, I never would have been able to make it this far. In college, as the fraternity president, I could get away with slacking, making excuses, laughing everything off as if it didn't matter. With the Young Republicans, I had always put on a good front, but when I was alone or with friends, I could revert to getting messed up, being hung over, and hating myself for doing it, although I wouldn't admit it. Now I was devoting all of my energy toward concrete goals. I had dreams to fulfill, and I had a feeling of forward motion most of the time.

No one is ever perfectly content, and I had bad days. My sense of success was often overshadowed, even though I was doing well. My divorce was a source of deep sadness, however, and I was still inviting unneeded drama into my life. I had to admit to myself that I was a drama king. I had never experienced a period in my life that lacked some sort of chaos. If there wasn't something going on already, I would create it. This was a vicious cycle that would continue on for some years to come. I wanted normalcy, but on the other hand, I didn't know what normalcy was. And there was still a nagging voice that would consistently pop up—sometimes out of the blue—telling me that I was destined to be a failure. My stepfather's words still rang in my ears. I still battled myself often, but I tried to fill my time and my mind with jumping over hurdles and making progress.

In the mindset of sobriety, I was forced to see myself as a man, for the first time, clearly. I had to face that man in the mirror. I never realized how tough that was until I did it consciously. I looked at myself, I saw beyond the simple reflection, and I made an effort to accept myself as I was. I knew that if I wanted to live in the world of my dreams, I had to love myself enough to do it. And I had to forgive myself and the people who had in some ways harmed me. I had to accept my greatness, which was all about being able to step into the person that God had designed me to be.

Chapter 4

Never Forget the Smell of Chorizo in the Morning

*Living a life of commitment and passion
requires walking, and sometimes crawling,
but never, ever giving up.*

· · · · · · · · · · ·

El Paso had served me very well. I had spread my wings there, and I had learned more about myself during that period than I had in a lifetime before. I was flourishing within the structure of Best Buy. I was proving what I was capable of, and I was being paid well for it. I was also enhancing my relationship with the Hispanic community. I was speaking in front of small groups like chambers of commerce and high schools, and I attended and acted as master of ceremonies at various events, some of which drew media coverage.

Work became something of a religion for me. I was rewarded there, although it seemed like the more I produced, the more Best Buy demanded. In 1996, the company flew me to Los Angeles to see if I might be interested in relocating there. They thought I had the right stuff to take over a new store, one of their first outside of Texas.

I couldn't think of a more exciting place to live, even though I'd never seen it before. I was single, ready, and willing. I wanted to be part of the growth; I wanted to be part of what Best Buy had to offer; I really wanted to live in Los Angeles! They had been very good to me so far, so I decided to make the move.

I really didn't know anything about Los Angeles or Orange County. Soon after I arrived, a colleague took me to dinner in Laguna Beach at Las Brisas. I thought I'd found heaven. Los Angeles was huge. First of all, I'd never been to a city that had so many freeways—the 10, the 91, the 60, the 405, the 101—and the number of cars in L.A. was astounding. The first time I asked for directions to Interstate 10, the guy looked at me like I was from Hicksville. The truth is, at that point, I was. L.A. had everything a person could possibly want, no matter the time or day of the week.

The diversity of the city was tremendous, with sections all over the city named for their residents: Chinatown, Japantown, Thaitown, Little Korea. Los Angeles also had one of the largest Latino communities in all the world. That really excited me. This was not the Los Angeles I'd seen in the movies—it was far more expansive and multicultural than I'd ever imagined. In a lot of ways, my move to L.A. proved to me just how naive I'd been about life in the big city. The lessons I learned would prepare me for what lay ahead, though. I tried to look on them as learning experiences, albeit frustrating ones.

Along with thirteen others, I was brought in as the general manager of a new store. This position gave me a chance to step up my career to the next level, and I was responsible for a lot of people. Best Buy gave me a mammoth 65,000-square-foot store. They expected the store to do 60 million dollars in annual revenue, almost three times the amount my current store made, and my staff would grow from the initial forty-five employees to over two hundred by the time we opened the store. I discovered that Best Buy had also given me the most difficult store in the city because of its location—close to Compton, in South L.A.

My store was in a Black neighborhood. Although I'd lived in Dallas, it was a culture shock. My staff was predominantly Black, which I admit intimidated me at first. No one should be judged by their ethnicity, but the only thing I'd ever heard about Compton at the time had to do with gangs and violence. I assumed that was the world I had entered, but I was wrong. True, some of my employees had gone through very hard times. Many of them were forced to sleep on their floors because bullets flew through the air at night where they lived. I never let anyone know that I was scared to go out to my car after the sun went down. Instead, I built alliances. I gave the police department a much-needed copier. I wanted them to respond when I called—and fast.

Before we opened, I had to hire more than two hundred employees. I took risks that I'm not sure the company appreciated. I always felt the need to reach out, and I had the chance to do so at this store. I often hired the unhirable. I understood by that time that second chances didn't come easily, especially if someone had gotten caught up in criminal activity. My own stepfather had barely escaped from a life of crime. I also knew firsthand what it felt like to be turned down for a job because of the color of my skin. My goal was to give back to the communities that Best Buy realized a profit from. It made perfect sense to me.

The residents of Malibu and Beverly Hills weren't applying for work in South L.A. Many of my employees had little or no experience, and some of them did, in fact, have a criminal record. Most of the time I didn't know that until later. For example, I was having lunch with an employee one day when he told me that he'd been arrested for several crimes and that he'd been a member of one of America's most notorious gangs, the Bloods. I asked him how he had passed our background checks, and he told me that as long as he stayed clean, the district attorney kept his records sealed.

My staff succeeded, though. In fact, they exceeded many of their goals under my management because I had done something different—I had demonstrated to them that I cared. I took time to get to know my employees: I asked them questions about their families, I asked what their desires were, and where they wanted to go in life. Obviously, this was a very different management style than I'd employed earlier. One of the benefits of working for a company like Best Buy was that they spent a lot of time and money training their managers, including me. Whenever I had a chance to take a class or a seminar and have the company pay for it, I was glad to go. I made great efforts to learn new skills and to improve my working relationships. During those many seminars, I began entertaining the idea of becoming a motivator or life coach myself.

I had some mishaps. Sometimes I trusted too much. I once chose an employee I thought I could trust to drive a van I had rented. One evening I got a frantic phone call from one of my managers: "Dan, you need to get over here right away! Shawn stole the van!" He was gone for two weeks. Finally his sister called and told me that her no-good brother was joy riding in my vehicle. She told me where he was, and I called the police. He was high as a kite when we arrived.

I was also learning how to love people for who they were. While I was trying to learn how to forgive myself, I began to look past the surface of the people I spent my days with. One of the stockmen, Cleveland, struck me as a very interesting fellow. He didn't live the kind of life most of us do. He was hard to understand, and he looked like he shared Don King's barber; but he clearly had a big heart. Cleveland surprised me one day. I would reward employees for meeting goals by taking them to lunch. Cleveland had surpassed his, so over lunch I learned that his dream was to open his own bakery. Judging by his appearance, that was the last profession I'd have thought of for him. "What would be your specialty?" I asked.

"I make the best peach cobbler in the world," he responded with the confidence of a top pastry chef. A week later, I threw a barbeque for the staff—it was a monthly event. Cleveland brought his peach cobbler. He hadn't been exaggerating. I told him that if he could put the same passion into his career as he put into his cobbler, he'd be a smashing success. He was promoted to management a few years later. He had just needed some encouragement.

We had to work very hard to open the store. With the deadline coming up, my employees put in long hours. We had just a couple of days before the doors opened, and we had so much inventory—the trucks just kept coming and coming—it seemed like we would never be able to get everything up on the shelves before our grand opening. On the eve of the big day, while we struggled to finish merchandising the store, I was forced to ask my staff to stay even longer. I was Hispanic, my management was White, and we managed a predominantly Black staff. Cultural differences had created tension along the way, but we weren't done with the job, and the doors were opening in the morning, no matter what. All of us felt exhausted already. A group of older employees refused to stay, though, demanding to go home in a manner I found inappropriate. They began dictating to me, in other words, how to manage them.

Without thinking, my instincts took over. I jumped up on the counter, towering above a bunch of very surprised people. I raised my voice so loud that a passerby outside probably could have heard me: "If you leave, don't come back. You won't have a job. If you want to be managed like children, you'll be managed like children. If you want to be managed like adults, you'll be managed like adults. Now, you make a choice. I don't care which one you make, but don't you dare walk back in that door if you leave me when I need you the most. The door's open. Go." Inside, I was petrified. I wasn't sure what I would do if they left. I was hoping they wouldn't call my bluff.

The management staff looked at me like I had just

handed them a death sentence. Nobody moved. They thought I'd lost my mind, and just stood there, dumbstruck. I lowered my voice, calmed myself, and told my staff that we would work for two more hours. I wasn't finished, though. Before I stepped down from the counter, the preacher in me took over, and I did my best to sell them all on the vision. I gave them a mini-sermon on how exciting it would be to know that all of us, as a team, had been able to accomplish something monumental. When I finally planted my feet back on the floor, they all quietly turned back and returned to work. We opened the store the next morning, on time.

On occasion, an employee would act flat out rude and tell me off: "This stinks; I'm not doing anything else," they'd say, and walk out the door. Some returned, begging to have their jobs back, and some I never saw again. It seemed like combat training at times. I had to learn how to take control, but more importantly, I had to learn to *stay* in control of the people who worked for me. In general, I remained focused and results-oriented. I enjoyed managing people, and I learned new strategies every day, not only in getting people to do what I wanted, but in encouraging them to do well for themselves. Everyone has a different way of relating, and I needed my employees to be my allies.

My new understanding of management included the realization that my job was to serve two different clients: the people who worked for me and the people who bought from me. I used the tools I had learned as a minister: compassion, understanding, and service. When I asked employees about their lives, they became people:

moms, dads, children, grandfathers, grandmothers, brothers, and sisters. We all had common ground. We were human. I wanted to make sure I gave my people what they needed, along with that crucial ingredient I was so familiar with: validation. I would tell them, "I'm here to serve you," although the truth is I think I had their respect from the moment I jumped up onto that counter.

• • • • • • • • • • •

Imagine the possibilities. Imagine where you might find yourself if you follow your heart.

• • • • • • • • • • •

In the same way I built alliances with the police department, I began extending myself in other directions as well. I threw an open house for city employees, including the fire department, city representatives, and the school system, and offered deep discounts. My goal was simple. I wanted to help them, and I wanted them to regard Best Buy as the place they would make all of their future purchases. I wanted everyone to feel like our goal was to provide the utmost satisfaction to the customers.

As I had in El Paso, I looked at the Hispanic community as an important part of the success equation for our store. I had always struggled with who I was, ethnically speaking. There's no doubt, I had something of an identity crisis. In El Paso, I had begun to feel like part of a culture, and there were many aspects of being a Latino that exhilarated me. My culture was rich in tradition, history, and potential. In Los Angeles, I made it a priority to tap into the city's Latino population.

Part of doing that meant making an effort to really understand the Latino culture in L.A., as opposed to the culture in Texas. Being Latino in L.A. is exciting because we have such a large population. In El Paso, I had mostly come across Mexicans and Mexican Americans. In L.A. there were Cubans, Mexicans, Puerto Ricans, Colombians, Ecuadorans, Guatemalans, Nicaraguans, El Salvadorans, and more. There were subcultures within subcultures. Until I moved to Los Angeles, I had never heard of Cesar Chavez and Si Se Puede. Latinos were proud here, and I was more than happy to fit in. In fact, I was very proud.

Beyond the day-to-day responsibilities of managing such a huge complex, I focused on giving things away, which made sense to Best Buy. They were wise to realize that happy customers kept coming back, and word of our generosity spread rapidly. I had no problem spending Best Buy's money on improving people's lives and surroundings. I knew that our store generated enough profits to make donations on a monthly basis. On our profit-and-loss statements, we had at least $1,000 a month to spend on community service projects. The district had $5,000. In my opinion, what we were giving was beans compared to the millions we made from the community.

On Christmas Eve I heard a story on the radio that touched me. A single mother had been robbed of all the gifts she had bought for her kids. I had the power to do something. It reminded me of when I'd been a kid, and the Salvation Army had acted as Santa. I called the station and asked them to contact the woman so that I could give her a computer, a washer, and a dryer. The managers of other stores didn't particularly share my sense of philanthropy—it meant less profit for them, and their bonus checks would then be lower. Me? I didn't care. It made me feel better to give than to earn a couple thousand dollars to spend on suits or another television for myself. I saw something bigger: I saw a potentially very powerful group of people who I strongly related to. If I could manage two hundred employees, could I lead part of the population? Could I be a driving force in people's lives? Could I become a minister of sorts, but not a minister of God? Could I reach into the depths of Latino minds and souls and lift them up? It was only a seed of an idea, but as all seeds do that land on fertile soil, it took root and slowly began to grow.

Chapter 5

A Look at the Man
in the Mirror

We can all reach greatness if we are
willing to deal with the curves
that life throws our way.

• • • • • • • • • • •

The president of Best Buy came to see me one day and
validated my opinion that no one at the company really
knew how difficult my store was to manage. I told him,
flat out: "This store is liking riding a bull. Sometimes
I'm on the bull's back and I'm doing okay. Sometimes
I'm riding his horns. Sometimes I'm on the bottom of
the bull riding his belly. And a lot of times, I'm just hang-
ing on to his tail. But I haven't let go."

After several years at Best Buy, though, I had grown
accustomed to my work, and I was champing at the bit
for new opportunities. Playing an important role in the
Latino community was paramount in my mind. Every
action begins with a dream, and I was beginning to form
some very big dreams.

Professionally, things were happening outside the
realm of my management position. Best Buy had al-

ready given me the opportunity to get involved in projects that involved the Latino community, and I had established many important relationships with various prominent community and political leaders. I must admit that I was surprised by how many successful Latinos there were in Los Angeles. I enjoyed my role as a Best Buy spokesperson more than any other work I'd done, and I was meeting helpful and interesting people in the Latino media, including several editors and writers at *La Opinion*, Los Angeles' premier Spanish-language newspaper; the television station Univision; the *Los Angeles Times*; and several radio stations.

In 1996, just a couple of months after I'd arrived in L.A., Univision asked me to participate in a special Christmas Eve talk show program. I was taken aback at first—the idea scared me, to be honest. Initially I didn't even give them an answer. Instead I thought of excuses. Lingering doubts reared up: "Who do you think you are? You can't do a TV talk show!" I had done some radio interviews in El Paso, but I'd never been on camera before. Like past challenges, though, I was able to convince myself that this was another opportunity to show the world what I could do. It was the busiest time of the year at the store, which limited my free time. Univision's solution was to tape the show, which meant that after a long day at the store, I'd head out to the studio.

The show's theme was "Latinos and the Christmas Holidays," and the panel consisted of a pastor, a psychologist, and myself. My role was to discuss the Hispanic community's retail buying habits and to give them helpful shopping tips. In truth, I hadn't been in Los

Angeles long enough to be able to provide any substantial commentary on the subject. My area of expertise was Best Buy and what we had to offer, so I decided to focus on the idea that shopping and giving gifts had lost importance. I wanted to encourage listeners to go "all out" this year, and to do it at Best Buy. I wanted to mention the name of the store as many times as possible, and I wanted to refer to our ninety-day price-match guarantee policy. Mistakenly, I declared that we were proud of our ninety-*month* policy. My boss laughed later. He said it was the only time he would be forced to deal with an ad campaign six years later.

Despite a bad case of nerves, I found that I really enjoyed working on camera—playing to the audience. It was something else to be proud of. Until then, I thought my efforts at work had been something anyone could do, but now I had stepped up a rung on the ladder. I was further convinced that by saying "yes" instead of "no," I could fulfill my quest to accept my own greatness. It was imperative to accept responsibilities and opportunities whenever and however they came. In the next few weeks, I was offered the chance to participate in several other events. A German television station came to interview me about the store, and I was presented with a key to the city of Hawthorne by the mayor. My efforts were paying off.

By saying "yes," I was paving a road for myself, and I was saying "yes" more and more. For one, Susanna Whitmore, who worked for *La Opinion*, asked me to participate in many Latino-themed events. I owe her a great deal of gratitude for taking me under her wing. The national sales manager of *La Opinion,* Robert Gordillo, also helped me to expand my career. I was very loyal to Best Buy, but at the same time I realized it really didn't matter who I worked for—this process had really become about *me.* Best Buy provided the vehicle, but I was using my own God-given talents. No one was instructing me as to what to say; I was out there winging it. I had "personality," people informed me. People spontaneously told me that they liked me. They listened to me, and they thought what I had to say was important and meaningful. It began to dawn on me that my particular talent lay in my ability to draw people to me. It had been happening since my college days, but it still hadn't yet sunk in. Most importantly, I felt that I could help bring about positive change. Why not? That's what I thought people were on earth to do. I had always felt that way.

I now knew the fundamentals of managing a very big company. I knew how to function in corporate America. But I wasn't good at everything. Like the best leaders, I knew enough to surround myself with good people. As I became more well-known, competitors began to court me, offering more money, along with signing bonuses. "Me? Little small-town-boy Danny?" I thought. At the same time, in the "city of the stars," I was being invited to various celebrity events, including a party at Universal City for the cast of *ER.* Many times, I had to pinch myself, wondering if I was dreaming.

The woman I was dating wanted more than anything to go to the daytime Emmys. She thought that since I was so "connected," I could surely get tickets. I wasn't a big fan of soap operas, but I knew who Susan Lucci was at least. I thought it was worth a shot. I'd always had a problem recognizing boundaries, but if you don't ask, you'll never know, I figured. I honestly didn't know better. I knew that Best Buy was spending millions of dollars on advertising, and I decided to use that as leverage. I called the corporate office. "Dan, you're asking for a lot," was the response. I didn't know at the time that the Emmys were mainly for industry types and their families.

"Look," I said, "it's Valentine's Day, and I'd love to take my girlfriend." They called me back with apologies, and I told my girlfriend the bad news. Then the day before the show, someone from one of the local TV news channels I had formed a friendship with called to ask if I wanted two tickets to the Emmys. Happy Valentine's Day, indeed! I bought my girlfriend a beautiful dress; I sprang for a tux, and we walked down the red carpet in Beverly Hills the next day. Susan Lucci actually went out of her way to compliment my girlfriend on her dress. It made my night, and I know it made hers. I was on top of the world. It was like Paris all over again. I felt like I belonged in Hollywood; I belonged in this lifestyle; I belonged with these people. I fit, although I was still little more than a fly on the wall.

· · · · · · · · · · ·

Shortly after the grand event, I found something out that really bothered me: The general managers I was training made more money than I did. I knew that to deal with this I would have to write a letter to corporate arguing my demonstrably greater worth. But I wasn't able to find the words to explain *why* I was worth more; I just *knew* I was. I've found that this is a very common dilemma for a lot of people. I hadn't yet learned how to articulate my thoughts and feelings. I never wrote the letter, but I did talk to my boss about more pay, although he said, "No."

Since I didn't feel appreciated at Best Buy, I began to pay more attention to the other companies wooing me. After six years with Best Buy, I felt I needed a change and decided to take a risk. I went to work for Office Depot. It wasn't about the money. The job they gave me was to take on one of their troubled stores and turn it around. That suited me perfectly. I felt that if I was going to take over a store, I wanted the toughest store in the district. Meeting challenges, I thought, honed my skills and proved my mettle, which worked in both positive and negative ways for me, since I was under the impression that everything had to be hard.

My personal life was about to get more complicated, too. On a romantic escapade, I flew to San Francisco with the woman I had taken to the Emmys, Renée, and after a ride in a luxurious limo, I proposed to her in a French restaurant. We decided to get married on a yacht. We'd had a rough start, the result of a very passionate relationship, and I still didn't really know who I was. I saw myself looking in from the outside, like a child, seeking acceptance. It must have been frustrating for her. When one half of a partnership is always seeking validation from the other half, it can easily come off as weakness.

Our relationship was out in left field, and it would soon take its toll on both of us. There was always too much drama. Renée was analytical, and I was very spontaneous; she needed security, but that was something I didn't hold much stock in. Just days before the wedding, we called it off. Although we were living together, I wasn't convinced that this was the best route to take, especially after my first experience with matrimony. I couldn't help but wonder if I deserved better. Maybe I deserved a woman who honored me. Renée went back to her ex-boyfriend.

At the same time, I also became frustrated with Office Depot. I knew I had made the wrong choice, and I regretted it. I was forever making the wrong decision. Luckily, Best Buy offered me a store in Albuquerque, and I accepted. I was grateful that they'd taken me back. But before I left, Renée changed her mind and persuaded me that marriage was our destiny. We eloped to Las Vegas before making the move to New Mexico. Now the tables would turn. Renée was an educated woman and grew unhappy in backwater Albuquerque. Now *she* deserved more. After a year, I was forced to choose between my marriage and my job. For the first time in my life, I compromised my career for a relationship.

I resigned from Best Buy, and we moved back to California, but within months we separated and divorced. I was distraught. I had come so far, and then I had lost it all in a period of a year. What had I done wrong? How could I learn to make solid choices and accept what was given to me? How could I have gone from the Emmys to nowhere so fast? Now, after my second divorce, I was forced to take a look at the common denominator. I knew that this failure wasn't all about her. I had to take responsibility for my own actions, and many of them had been bad ones—ill-informed and done out of desperation for approval.

What I really wanted was more out of life. I was now broken mentally, emotionally, and physically. I had come to the end of my rope. I started drinking again because it was my way of escaping, and because I forgot the lesson of the Europeans to savor instead of guzzle. I was headed down a street I was very familiar with: self-destruction.

This time, though, I wanted the merry-go-round to stop almost right away. My life so far had been a whirlwind; I'd constantly been at odds with myself. I was simultaneously pursuing and running from my own success and accomplishments. It was hard work! At age thirty-something, it was time I took an uncompromising look at reality. Broken, alone, and lost, I began a deep exploration of myself. I took a look at the man in the mirror.

· · · · · · · · · · ·

When I'd made the decision to move back to Los Angeles to save my marriage and given up my job with Best Buy, the company had no general manager positions available there, and I refused to take anything less. The situation added to my state of inner siege. I had worked very hard at Best Buy, and I had earned the respect of my peers as well as that of the CEO of the company, Dick Schultz, and its VP, Ken Weller. I admired both men; they had been instrumental in my professional development. But I had been determined to put my wife's needs before my own, and I had walked away from a fortune in stocks and salary. In my mind, at least, I thought I had behaved nobly, if a bit foolishly.

CompUSA hired me in September of 1998. I was given a store that made $300,000 a month, and I soon took it to $1.3 million a month, which resulted in a number of awards. If there was one thing for sure, I was a whiz at work, no matter how troubled my personal life was. In spite of all the pain, I still showed up, except for the day I went into my office, shut the door, and cried. I was truly heartbroken; I was lonely; I was emotionally defeated; I was done. My pain was overwhelming, my stomach turning over and over because, just like Ziggy had shown me several years before, I knew I had no one to blame but myself. I was the common denominator. I was the only one who was always involved in my life—there was nobody else.

My snap decision was to leave everything behind. It was a pivotal moment in my life. I could drink, I could even snort coke. I could just disappear. Instead I picked up my briefcase and went to the Crystal Cathedral in Garden Grove, California. Little did I know it would become my haven. I walked into the foyer and approached a security guard. "I need to speak to a pastor right away," I said. He shook his head no and told me that visits were by appointment only. I had two choices: I could go get a beer or I could plead my case. Trammell Crowe's private secretary would have been proud. Only this time, I meant it from the depths of my soul.

Finally Bob Cavender, the head of the men's ministry, came down to see me. He invited me up to his office, where I cried right in front of him for an hour. Between sobs, I told him my life story. I told him that I had learned from childhood to be strong and self-sufficient, but my personal life was crumbling around me. I had no faith in myself. I had, for so many years, held in the pain of all the crazy mistakes I had made. I was literally holding myself hostage. Now, in front of this kind stranger, I let it all out. When I had exhausted myself, I simply got up and said, "Sir, thank you so much. Now I've got to go back to work. I have a business to run. I've got people waiting for me."

I finished out my work day in a daze. Something in me had shifted. As I made my way home, I felt relieved in a strange way. Back at the apartment, I picked up a copy of Cheri Huber's book, *That Which You Are Seeking Is Causing You to Seek*. It had been my ex-wife's book, and it really made an impression on me as I paged through, exhausted by the day's events. Her theory— that joy is not defined by a trophy wife, an awesome job, a fancy car, or wealthy friends—really spoke to me. True joy, Huber wrote, is compassion turned inward; the end of struggle; the end of competition! My job was to look deeper—beyond the surface. I simply had to focus on the qualities God had given me, and I had to avoid looking for happiness in the material world.

By letting my guard down with Bob, I'd marked the first step on my path to healing, to forgiveness, to acceptance, and to power. It would be the first day of a new internal journey, one on which I would learn to stop competing against myself. Finally, after struggling for so long, I could begin taking baby steps to a healthier way of life, both for me and for those around me. That first baby step—going to the Crystal Cathedral—ultimately saved my life and led me forward. Clearly there was a bad side of life and a good side; I had to make the choice. It wasn't the first time I'd realized that fact, but it was the first time I would act on it daily. Running was no longer an option. I had to learn some lessons, one of which was that I had to be grateful. I had ability; I had drive and tenacity; I had the determination to be more than what I was. I just had to accept *who* I was.

· · · · · · · · · · ·

In the next few weeks, I moved into a new apartment in Orange County and continued to work for CompUSA. I reached out to some of the people I had abandoned, and I began to attend events, including a "who's who" party at the Getty Museum, one of the most marvelous examples of modern architecture, in the beautiful Santa Monica Mountains. I found myself surrounded by smart, successful, important Latinos. It reminded me what my potential was. I redoubled my efforts to keep moving forward.

Meanwhile, I attended a divorce- and grief-recovery group at the Crystal Cathedral. I needed to be with people who would just accept me for myself, and this time I was smart enough to do it. The healing process had begun in earnest. Dr. Robert Schuller, the pastor there, offered guidance that especially moved me: "If it is going to be, it is up to me." Sunday after Sunday, I sat in his congregation, listening closely to his sermons and taking notes like a madman. I vowed that some day I would share the stage with him, and I would thank him for his crucial words of encouragement during my darkest days.

I also went to a therapist after experiencing a period of sleeplessness that lasted over a month. I felt weak, and my mind wandered continuously. My therapist put it plainly, saying, "You need to rest." Taking drugs concerned me, so I refused to take sleeping pills. He replied, "I don't think you have a choice. It's either the pills or the hospital." I swallowed my pride and accepted the medication. That first night I slept for fourteen hours. I needed to rejuvenate. Exhaustion, starvation, and loneliness make introspection impossible. These were immediate things I had to address.

The holidays were coming up and I dreaded them. Instead of wallowing, though, I went on my first church mission trip to an orphanage just across the border in Mexico. I thought it would be a very sad trip, but it became the highlight of my year. I was able to step outside of myself and see people who existed on almost nothing for who they really were. These people were hurting, yet they were happy.

On our way home from a side trip, a little boy asked me, "Sir, are you rich?"

"No, son, I'm not," I answered. He had a bunch of marbles in his hand that he was very proud of. I identified with him because when I was his age, marbles were the only things we could afford to play with. He was proud of them, and I understood why.

He asked me again, "Sir, are you rich?"

I smiled and said, "No, son, I'm not. I'm just an ordinary man—just like everyone else. But here, take this."

I reached into my pocket and gave him my change. I felt very good about giving him the change. It made me feel good to give him the money but sad that I couldn't do more.

He smiled at me and said, "Thank you."

The next day, as I reached down to put on my $200 Gucci loafers, it occurred to me that he probably didn't even own a pair of shoes. I guess that did make me rich, at least relatively speaking. When I drove up to the Crystal Cathedral that afternoon, I remembered that this boy attended church in a tent or garage. We saw the church on our mission trip, and it was very humble: a makeshift construction of boards and rocks they put together and called a church. That boy had been very proud of what he had, though. I had to admire him.

This period in my life was about proactively seeking peace and spirituality, finding myself, and setting up my future. But the process took years, not weeks or months. One of the most important things I learned was that I had to be willing to do the homework to find personal success. It wasn't until I was ready to do that work that my own doors of perception opened. I had to stay the course. I had discounted myself and my achievements so readily and for so long. Now I allowed myself to begin dreaming again. I was ready to accept my mission in life, although I still wasn't sure what it was. I knew there would be problems; I knew I would make mistakes; I knew I still had a streak of self-sabotage. Even after my hard work and the support of so many others, I had to admit that I still had a tendency to look for ways to fail.

I resumed journaling, something I had found com-
forting in the past. The process made sense to me. I also
wrote poetry. In both I connected with myself and the
creative side of my being that I had buried a long time
ago—that sensitive side of me that loved art and people.
Most of this writing took place at the divorce-recovery
group; it was the only place where I could really slow
down and focus. I began asking myself questions. What
had contributed to my beliefs about myself? What made
me want to run from everything? Was I as bad as I had
made myself out to be in my own mind?

When a student is ready, a teacher will appear. Mine
came in the form of Dr. Sande Herron, whom I met at
the Crystal Cathedral. Sande acted as a pastor for the
Crystal Cathedral singles group and had a doctorate
degree in psychology. When the divorce- and grief-recovery group ended, I wasn't sure where to go next. Our
counselor recommended that we visit the singles group.
I decided to attend the group for those fifty years and
older, although I was only thirty-five. I felt safe there. I
wasn't really looking for a romantic relationship. During my first meeting, Sande walked over to me, placed
her hand on my cheek, and said, "I love you." My heart
melted. I longed for affection, for someone to reach out.
With just a touch of her hand, I felt like we already knew
each other. My reaction was to cry, and she sat down to
talk with me. I felt a direct and strong connection immediately, and we became fast friends.

One night after an event where I'd shared the story of
my divorce, Sande asked me to come to her office to
chat. It was a friendly gesture, which I happily embraced,

and we started talking. Soon we made our talks a habit. One day, she said, "Danny Boy, you have talent, and I truly believe that you have the potential to be one of the great speakers of our country, as good as Anthony Robbins. I want to spend time with you, and I won't charge you. I don't have to do this, but I want to because I am drawn to you. As long as you continue to have faith in our friendship, I will continue to try and guide you."

From then on, I went to Sande whenever I felt confused or scared. I knew that God had sent Sande into my life to help me recover. She was my friend, my confidante, and my second mother, all wrapped into one wonderful package. Sande offered me unconditional acceptance and encouragement, which I doubted at first. I walked out of her office many times, thinking she was plain crazy. What did she see in me that I just couldn't? Over the months to come, her team of singles would love me back to health, as if they'd found an abandoned baby boy. They loved me during bad times; they loved me during good times; they continually reached out to me. I returned the favor as best I could. We filled each other's empty spaces.

Then that summer, on the Fourth of July, I went out with a friend for a beer. We ended up having a few. On the way home, I stopped to buy something to eat. Continuing down the road, when I reached over to pick up my food from the front seat, I swerved, right in front of a cop. I ended up in jail, booked for drunk driving. I felt lower than an ant's belly. How could I have done so much healing and end up in this disastrous situation? What was it about me that made me continue to sabotage myself? I was too embarrassed to call anyone, so I just stayed until they let me go. It was a slap in the face. Everything had been going so well, but I had screwed it up again.

For the next year, no one knew that I just sat at home because I'd lost my driver's license. But I went a bit easier on myself than I had in the past, when I would have fed my own grief and shame and multiplied them with negative thinking. "I'm human," I told myself. "I make mistakes. I'll never be perfect, and failure is a part of life." To lie down and not get up again was utterly unthinkable. I vowed to keep "showing up" no matter how painful it got. I understood that my own decisions had dictated the position in which I found myself.

In time, facing failure actually lent me strength. I began to understand that life wasn't happening *to* me, it was happening *for* me, and I had a choice either to learn from my experiences or not. After all, everything I had become I had learned by falling down and getting up again. My job was to avoid repeating my mistakes. I learned that some failures were even okay. There was always another day to start over again. Zig Ziglar once said, "Failure is an event." Driving drunk, although I wasn't proud of it, had been an event. It hadn't been "Dan." I took responsibility for it, but the event didn't represent the real me. I was not the event.

Without the ability to drive, I was unable to work steadily. I went from job to job for a while. I knew what I was inspired to do, but I was still too afraid. I wanted to speak to people, I wanted to coach and write and inspire people. I questioned myself constantly. I felt as if my education was lacking, and I said so to a group of people who happened to have Ph.D.'s. Sande said, "Daniel, you may not have graduated from college, but you are wise enough to seek guidance. That's why you are in a room full of Ph.D.'s." But who was I to think I could be a motivator, an empowerment specialist? All I knew was that I had an overwhelming need and desire to tell my story so that others could learn from it. I knew that it would release me from my past, and I knew that I could lend comfort and encourage people all over the world. I could show everyone how to accept their own individual greatness, if given the chance. But who would give me that opportunity?

Sande helped me out by offering me the chance to speak at singles meetings at the Crystal Cathedral. I was nervous, but I got a great response every time. Like others before her, Sandy told me, "You're a natural! When you speak, people listen!"

Chapter 6

Accepting and Stepping into My Greatness

Many people would secretly like for us to fail. The key to success is looking for the yes's in life rather than the no's.

• • • • • • • • • • •

Over the next few years, Sande worked with me to make me a better speaker and guided me tirelessly. More than anything else, she wanted me to embrace my innate talents—the ones that lay deep inside, inaccessibly deep. We met every week, sometimes twice a week, and I learned to allow her to tell me what I needed to hear so desperately—that I was a good person and that I was loved. She never told me what I *wanted* to hear, just what I *needed* to hear.

More and more groups asked me to speak, usually through small business and community organizations. I found that there were literally thousands of people hungry for sustenance in the form of an empowering message. At one point, Sande invited me to attend a meeting of the National Speakers Association. Part of her mentoring involved surrounding me with other speakers and coaches. This invitation followed a session with her where she told me that she thought she had taken me as far as she could. I had to find another, more experienced coach who was out on the circuit and who could help me to advance more quickly. It was almost like she wanted to kick me out of the nest and force me to fly. I felt very disappointed at first, but I came around to seeing her logic soon enough.

The National Speakers Forum was a watershed event for me and led me to one of the most defining moments of my life, although it took time to become apparent. One of the featured speakers that day was Nancy Vogl, the president of the Universal Speakers Bureau in Lansing, Michigan. When Nancy took the stage, she began by telling the story of how she had gotten involved in the business of representing speakers. She described one of the first events she ever put together—a motivational forum. In her desire for success, she said, she had told everyone that Dr. Wayne Dyer, a very successful writer and teacher, was slated to be the keynote speaker. She paused and smiled, and then she told us that she had gotten herself into quite a predicament: She had sold out the event before she had gotten a commitment from Dr. Dyer. I sat on the edge of my chair as I listened to the story. Nancy had a wonderful ability to capture an audience's attention. She didn't even know Wayne Dyer, she said, and she became terribly nervous, wondering how she was going to pull it off. In the end, she relied upon her confidence and her gift of persuasion, and she'd been fortunate enough to get Dyer on the phone. Fifteen minutes later, she had him convinced.

He agreed to show up at her event. She described it as one of the greatest moments of her life.

Nancy went on to tell us that because of her success with the event, her friend and mentor, Og Mandino, suggested that she devote her energy to creating the speakers bureau. When she mentioned Mandino's name, I gasped out loud. He had been one of the first motivational authors I had read, and his work had left a huge impression on me. *The Greatest Salesman in the World* had been instrumental in my desire to be a motivational speaker myself. I wanted to do what Mandino did: motivate and inspire the world!

When Nancy finished speaking, at least a hundred people rushed the stage to talk to her. I decided that I would take some time to gather my thoughts and send her an e-mail later. I went back to my apartment and spent the rest of the day thinking about what she had shared. In essence, she had taken a huge risk and had won big. It cemented my belief that I could only get what I wanted by taking risks that were beyond my comfort zone. All along, Sande had told me I had what it took. Was I ready to believe that? Was I ready to believe in myself, once and for all? Could Sande have the foresight that I had lacked all this time? Could she see my future better than I could myself?

When ready, I sat down and composed an e-mail to Nancy, mostly to let her know that her story had intrigued and moved me. I began by telling her that I simply wanted to thank her. I had noticed in her printed material that she discouraged e-mails and "audition" videos to Universal Speakers Bureau unless requested.

I didn't want her to think I was trying to pitch her. Instead I wrote about the influence Og Mandino had had on me, and that although I'd never had the pleasure of hearing him in person, I was very fond of his books. I added that she had given me hope regarding my path, even though I still wasn't absolutely clear what that path was.

For a couple of weeks I didn't hear anything from her. I really didn't expect to. Then, one day, I opened my e-mail and saw her name in my inbox. In her note, she asked for my address because she wanted to send me something. That really piqued my curiosity. I was very excited. Like a kid anticipating Christmas morning, I waited anxiously to see what the surprise would be.

It was, in fact, the Christmas season, and I had spent the past weeks literally sitting on my couch wondering where I was going to go with my career. World's Greatest Motivator: The words continually passed through my head. There were many nights I was unable to sleep because a fiery inner voice rang through my mind. "Step into your greatness, Dan," it called, over and over again. At times, I had actually prayed that this passion, this fire, would go away, but it never did. In fact, it only got stronger.

At the same time I was struggling about what to do with my life, a miraculous and wonderful event occurred. Relationships had not always been my strong suit, but I met a beautiful young woman named Monica, and we fell in love. Shortly after our relationship began, she informed me that she was pregnant. To say that I was shocked would be an understatement, but I'd always been of the mind that life provides mysterious surprises to teach us lessons and to help us become better people. I had always avoided even thinking about becoming a parent because of the negative examples I'd been exposed to as a child. I'd always felt I lacked the skills necessary to raise a child, and I doubted that I would be a good father. But Monica and I decided that having this baby was the right thing to do. It had meaning, and we felt as if we had been chosen to care for and love this particular child. I was determined to face up to all of these new and admittedly frightening responsibilities. I was excited, but I was terrified. I had to ask myself, "What kind of father would I be? Could I be different than my own father and stepfather had been?" I knew one thing for sure: I would always lead by example. If I was not willing to follow my dreams and passions, how could I expect my son to? I had deep faith in Monica, and I resolved to allow this blessing to change me for the better. I didn't know then just how many amazing changes were in my near future.

While the upcoming birth of my son occupied my mind, on a cold winter morning I received a package from Lansing. I was almost afraid to open the box. Here I was, agonizing over what I should do with my life, which direction to go in, and then, Bam!, there it was. As if in slow motion, I opened the box and extracted a letter.

Dear Daniel:

This is a numbered and autographed Heirloom edition of three of Og Mandino's famous books. Six thousand sets were produced, but before Og died in

September of 1996, he had signed less than 3400 sets. I own all the last remaining copies of these sets, just a few dozen. I'll explain later how I came to acquire them.

You may already know Og's story, but here it is again to remind you: Og Mandino was an author, speaker, and former editor of *Success* magazine. When he was growing up, his mother always said that he would be a famous author and that she wanted him to go to college to fulfill his dream of writing. Three weeks after he graduated from high school, his mother died suddenly. Instead of going to college, Og went into the service and then into business. Eventually, hard times befell him, and he fell into depression and became lost in alcohol. He lost his home, his job, and his wife and daughter left him. Og crisscrossed the country working odd jobs and drinking heavily. One day, during a cold morning rain in Cleveland, he spied a handgun in the window of a pawn shop. The price tag said $29.00. He had just $30.00 in his pocket and the temptation was great. Og says he doesn't know what happened outside that store. All he remembered is that he "turned away from the pawn shop window, walked up the street in the rain, and staggered into a welcome shelter that was warm and dry . . . the public library." There he found comfort and hope in a little book by W. Clement Stone, entitled *Success Through a Positive Mental Attitude.*

It always amazes me how even allowing one positive sentence into our minds can change our entire lives. Og was so inspired by Stone's message that he inhaled his words and breathed them daily. He became a successful salesman, fell in love with a lovely woman named Bette, and was promoted to sales manager of an insurance company. Yet the dream his mother instilled in him to be a writer kept surfacing.

Finally, as he would write later, "I rented a typewriter and wrote a sales manual on how one could be better at selling insurance to the people in rural

areas using W. Clement Stone's success principles.
After rewriting it many times, I typed it as neatly as I
could, bound it all in a brown folder, and mailed it to
Mr. Stone's home office in Chicago, with prayers that
someone back there might actually read my work
and realize what great writing talent they had, buried
in Northern Maine."

Needless to day, someone did, and he went to
Chicago to write sales promotional material, later
becoming editor of Napoleon Hill and W. Clement
Stone's magazine titled *Success Unlimited* (now
known as *Success* magazine).

During his tenure at *Success Unlimited*, Og wrote a
little parable entitled *The Greatest Salesman in the
World*. The book's popularity began humbly, but it
would eventually become the biggest selling self-help
book in the world. Written in 1967, it still sells, to
this day, over 1.2 million copies every year!

Og would write twenty books in his lifetime, and
he became a much sought-after public speaker. The
most popular speech he delivered was on the Greatest Secrets of Success, and all who were ever privi-
leged to hear him were touched by his gentle
demeanor and simple, yet powerful message. He
always started out his presentation by saying, "I'm
just a writer."

I first heard Og speak in the mid-1980's. It was my
birthday that year, December 3rd, and Og was my
birthday gift to myself. I had just gone through a
horrible divorce and was left to raise my three little
girls alone. I had little spirit, no joy, was very short of
self-esteem, and definitely short on money. But Og's
message awakened something in me, and my life has
never been the same. This is why I proudly share
with everyone the philosophy on which I built my
little business. Our Bureau was born of love and
respect for the spoken word and the impact a single
message can have on a life . . . for a day, for a lifetime, even generations.

If it hadn't been for Og Mandino, I would not be
doing what I am doing now. Surrounded by wonder-

ful human beings who touch hearts, minds, and souls. It is so gratifying to know that I am connecting messengers of hope, substance, and spirit to people needing answers. I see myself as a "connector."

This Heirloom edition originally sold for $129.00 before Og died, and when he passed away, they were being sold for four times that amount. I acquired all of the last remaining autographed sets, such as the one you now own, when I bought out the bureau that represented Og. I sold a couple of sets initially, but then, one day, a magical thing happened.

I was in a restaurant in Los Angeles a couple of years a ago with my middle daughter, Monika. She and I were talking, and for some reason the conversation drifted. One of us, I don't know which one, mentioned the name "Og Mandino." Just as his name came up, a waiter was walking behind me delivering food to a nearby table. He stopped cold, spun around, and asked how we knew Og Mandino. I proceeded to tell him what I did for a living and how Og became a mentor to me. He had this elated look on his face and said, "I'll be right back!" He brought a young woman over to our table, introducing her as the hostess, but also as his wife. When she found out my relationship to Og, she just stood there with tears welling up in her eyes. She proceeded to tell us how reading Og's books had sustained her through some challenging times, and that if it hadn't been for his messages, she might not have made it.

When I got back to Michigan, I looked at all those books I had stacked on the shelves, and I just knew I couldn't sell them. Og writes in *The Greatest Miracle in the World* about a "ragpicker" . . . a label for someone who picks up junk; but in Og's book, a "ragpicker" refers to someone who "seeks more valuable materials than old newspapers and aluminum beer cans." Og's ragpicker sought out "waste materials of the human kind, people who still have great potential but have lost their self-esteem and their desire for a better life." I guess in a way I became one of Og's ragpickers. I sent that waiter and his hostess wife a set of these books, and I have not sold a set of them since.

I am slowly giving them away for special reasons or for no reason at all. The only requirement I have in my mind is that they go to people I know will appreciate them beyond just their binding and who are committed to rising above mediocrity.

When I got your e-mail, Daniel, I knew that one of these sets belonged to you. I don't know what it is you are struggling with, but I do know that Og is smiling down at you and would be very proud of you. Follow your heart and dreams!

I was more amazed than I'd ever been in my life after reading Nancy's generous words. I touched the books, almost as if they were fragile works of treasured art. Then I began to cry. I cried for what seemed like days. But I was not crying out of sadness; my tears came from the knowledge that I was finally convinced of what I needed to do. I finally understood that it wasn't up to me to decide *how* to make my dream come true, but to believe in my dream enough to step into it.

I had been to a Peter Lowe conference a few months back at the Anaheim Pond, and I had been astonished by what I'd seen. It was my first time at a forum so large; it looked like there were at least 10,000 people there. I was mightily impressed that so many people had come to experience a motivational seminar. People were obviously in need. Speakers that day included Bob Dole as well as many other prominent American leaders, both men and women. I sat there in the midst of all these people, and I had one overriding thought. The audience was a very diversified group of people, yet there wasn't a single Latino speaker or leader on stage. For that matter, there were no African Americans, Asian Americans, or Native Americans. I couldn't help but wonder whether there simply weren't any leaders out there to ask to participate.

I had a hard time focusing on the speakers, because my inner voice was practically screaming at me: "Daniel! Create a forum like this for Latinos!" And, of course, that voice was accompanied by another: "Who am I to create a forum like that?" It was as if I had a committee fighting with each other in my head. I simply had to overcome the negative and let the positive voice take over.

I focused like never before on following the invaluable advice and encouragement I had received from so many sources. When I got home, I made a decision that no one would ever be able to dissuade me from. I decided that if no one else was going to do it, then it was up to me. I would create an event. It would look like the monumentally successful forum I had just experienced, but it would be *for* Latinos *by* Latinos. At that moment, I had a crystal clear picture in my mind of Patty Crane. I smiled. "You can do it, Dan!"

That was before I had received my package from Nancy. My excitement had been so strong, but over the days and weeks to follow, I had allowed my grandiose plans to diminish. I had let my energy wane. Everything changed after I read Nancy's letter, however. It had come at a perfect time. While I paged through Og Mandino's brilliant books and thought about Nancy's motivating words, I had to take time to digest the magnitude of what I was about to embark upon. Now I knew it was not just a desire; it was a duty. I, Daniel Gutierrez, would create an event that would uplift and encourage thousands . . . maybe millions someday.

I couldn't wait to talk to Sande the next day and give her the news. I walked up to her office feeling queasy, though. It was unlike any feeling I had experienced before, which told me how important it was—and how different. I stepped through the door and said, "Sande, I'm ready."

"Ready for what," she asked in surprise.

"I'm ready to step into my greatness. I'm ready to be the speaker and motivator that you have told me for the last few years I can be. I am ready to accept the talent that God has given me. I'm ready to follow my heart."

"Daniel," she said, "what brought this about?"

"A miracle," I replied. "And so I will give a miracle in return. I am going to create the first Latino success forum in history. I know that the Latino community needs visible role models who will inspire greatness in our community. I want to be the person to bring it to them."

PART TWO

MOVING
MOUNTAINS
AND MAKING
IT HAPPEN

Chapter 7

Diary of a Man on a Mission

*Every day you win, you win for the entire
Latino community.—Xitlalt Herrera*

• • • • • • • • • • •

Over the following months, I hunkered down and focused all of my energy on making my dream a reality. I
made the decision to leave the corporate world behind,
and I created my own business—a company called Daniel
Gutierrez and Associates—which would provide me with
a structure for what I hoped would be a series of very
successful seminars directed at Latinos throughout the
United States and beyond.

I rented an office and began publishing information
about our goals, and I went on a networking frenzy. I
wanted everyone to know about my mission, and I
wanted everyone to see the merit of participating in my
dream. In the meantime, I was also using the skills I
had learned at Best Buy to do some outside consulting
work. After all, managing a $60 million business had
taught me a great deal, and I could in turn offer that

knowledge to small businesses to help them grow, increase sales, or manage their employees in better ways. While I was building my dream, it was a good way to pay the bills and keep moving forward. It also gave me the opportunity to meet people who would later play a role in my future endeavors. I coached individuals as well on matters concerning their business and personal lives. It gave me great gratification that I was able to practice, examine, and employ my own philosophies while giving people the help they needed. I've heard it said that we teach what we need to learn the most. It was certainly true for me.

· · · · · · · · · · ·

Journaling has always been a helpful tool for me. It allows me to take the time necessary to analyze and evaluate my thoughts and actions. I see things from new angles, and new ideas grow and flourish. Sometimes it's just a method of decompressing. By the end of 2001, my life—everyone's life—had changed profoundly. The United States had been attacked by a network of madmen, who, in one fell swoop, had led us to question our very security—our future. I wasn't going to let them hold me back, however dangerous the world seemed. People needed hope and encouragement more than ever now, and I would provide it for them. I would not be deterred by anyone. Imagine 2002 was a reality. The next year would be the longest, the busiest, the most exciting, the most disappointing, the scariest, the most thrilling, and the craziest of my life. My journal entries describe it best.

November 8, 2001

I'm keenly aware of being in a paralyzed state. I'm starting to notice this in people I do business with, and hints
of it in myself. People get so paralyzed that they don't
see the end result. They don't see how to get out of the
dilemmas they're in. It's almost like being in quicksand:
Doing nothing is good, and moving causes you to sink.
I got so paralyzed a while back that everything else
around me was paralyzed, too. Everyone was stressed
and felt uncomfortable. My assistant said recently about
that period, "I was scared you were going to quit. I knew
you were under an enormous amount of pressure." I
said, "No, I'll never quit. But I may take some time to
see where I'm at." At the time, I was looking at $30,000
due by the end of the month.

Today I'm a little bit clearer about what the right move
is: It's not to sit. Sometimes sitting still is good, but
being paralyzed is never good. I recognize that even in
my personal life, when I'm challenged and things aren't
going my way, I have to stop and keep going forward at
the same time.

I have signed contracts with Time Warner, we have
press releases going out, and we have Univision still
thinking about participating, looking for some contrac-
tual agreements. I'm under a lot of pressure. Quitting is
not an option, so I have to find ways to get people to
commit.

I realize that financially I'm in the position I'm in because I'm keeping myself back. I really need to be more
open, more willing to get help. I'm scared of losing part
of my business—losing this dream. I need to look at

other opportunities that can fund this process while I wait for corporate sponsors. At the same time, I have to push corporate sponsors to give me answers. For a month, I have expected my marketing team to do it. But it's my job.

November 13, 2001

Our press releases are going out next week. I'm calling Hewlett-Packard to force them to step up to the plate. I still believe they're going to give us the money, no matter what. I need to step back into the process, and that's what's beautiful about going forward and about believing and staying the course.

I've decided to bring on more people. When it comes to realizing a dream, the vision has to be shared with more than just one person or two people, or even three people who are willing to work to get you where you want to go. At this point, I feel that I've gotten as far as I can go alone. The Catch 22 is: I'm damned if I do and damned if I don't. I don't have the money to pay people, yet I know I can create the money if I can sign them on.

I've decided to take another risk by bringing on a new marketing firm, a very small mom-and-pop outfit. I thought it could be very beneficial in helping me get out into the community. I also need some rest. Suffering is optional, and so is sleep. But lack of sleep and lack of rest can keep a captain from being able to make the right decisions. I've found that when I'm tired and hungry I tend not to make the best decisions.

What accomplishments I have made, though! What strides I have made toward my vision of being true to myself and understanding what I'm all about. I'm still scared to death. Let the truth be known. Letting people in has created opportunities for me to do what I do best. I want to bring people together. I realize that I can create a powerful engine. I want to change the Latino community. I want everyone to walk out of Imagine 2002 feeling like they have gotten the words they have wanted and needed, powerfully spoken by people we have chosen. Am I a motivator or am I a motivator?

November 20, 2001
Heading back to my office today after a two-hour meeting with Univision's general manager, who is in charge of New York, Chicago, and Los Angeles, I was feeling powerful. I told them my vision and what I wanted to do. Heck, I told them what I need! Univision asked me a thousand questions, and I answered every one with confidence. I'm in the driver's seat. Sometimes I forget that. One of the most powerful TV stations in the Hispanic market could be a media partner for me! Staying the course has paid off. It would have been easy for me to give up and not believe. It's overwhelming and wonderful, all at the same time. I gave Time Warner a budget, and they have agreed. That's a rush.

Yesterday I visited a new production company. I won't end up using them, but at least I got a chance to share my vision. It's good practice. It's been a couple of packed days, too. I have to stay the course, follow through on the commitment, and avoid mediocrity. Life is still challenging, I'm pushing, but most importantly, I'm actually having a great time pursuing my dream and telling people about it.

I celebrated my two successes by speaking at the Crystal Cathedral singles event. I decided I was going to let it all out. I spoke from confidence; I spoke from conviction; I spoke from the depths of what I believe. Someone I respect very much told me afterward, "You have taken another step." I told her, "I am so ready to step out there and claim what is mine, to step out there and give hope to people who need it."

Another friend put it more metaphorically: "Dan, I admire you. I admire you because you took a dive off the highest board into a pool with no water, believing that the water would be there. And you had no safety net." I let that sink in. Just for a moment I thought, "Did I do that?"

The Taliban have retreated from Kabul, and the war looks better. Who knows if it's over or not. The bottom line is that things are getting better. The stock market seems to be an aberration—a testament that circumstances out of our control exist and will continue to exist until the end of time.

Yesterday I went to the L.A. Convention Center for a Latin Business Association conference. I hooked up with a guy from Solomon Smith Barney, who has a database of over 6,000 professional Latinos. He said he'd gladly help us promote Imagine. He also invited me to the Dorothy Chandler Pavilion tonight to meet some people from New York who might talk to me about sponsorship for the Hispanic Scholarship Fund.

The highlight of my day, though, was finding a new teacher—Moctesuma Esparza. He is one of the best Hispanic film producers in Hollywood with hits like *Selena* and *The Milagro Beanfield War.* My marketing team put the meeting together, and I felt like Moctesuma and I connected on a deep spiritual level. He asked me about my vision and my goals. I told him I'd be happy if one person was actually moved by what I have to say.

I'll never forget how he answered me. "Dan, may I repeat what you just said? You said you would be happy if one person changed as a result of your event. Dan, why do you sell yourself short? You have the opportunity to change all of humanity through the Latino community! That's the power you have!" I just sat there, unable to say a word. It was a lot for me to take in.

I never got around to the idea of him supporting the event, although I asked him to be a speaker and he agreed. It excited me just to be in his presence because of his great wisdom and spiritual aura. He asked me to call him. I woke up the next morning overwhelmed, literally crying, about what has been happening. In my worn-out clothes, simply the way I am, things are happening.

December 2, 2001

December hasn't been easy so far. The most disappointing thing is the number of people who won't support me, or even buy a ticket. Usually they are people who I have given my time freely to. I want to lash out, but how can I? All I can do is remove myself from the emotion and say, "Okay, what's next?"

When you're chasing your dream and things are tough, especially in December, it makes it very difficult to think straight. I am overwhelmed with the bills, with getting this project to work, and with ticket sales. There's even more stress than normal because of the holidays; the extra pressure of having a son and wanting to be the right kind of dad for him; the extra pressure of wanting not to struggle and yet to be deeply in the middle of creating this success forum for Latinos. I know this time of year is hard on people. My health is deteriorating: My stomach has been in pain, and my body and mind need rest. Only I'm not in a position to do that right now.

My rent is due and I don't have the money. My car payment is overdue. My administrative assistant is waiting to get paid. I don't have the money. My child support needs to be paid. I never want to feel like my son is a burden, but I get tired. It's got nothing to do with him; it's got to do with the money, and money is tight. The proverbial cupboard is bare. I know that my attitude has to change. I really believe that I can change everything by being positive and believing. I have to focus and make decisions that are good for the business—to make it through the next weeks. One good thing is that my Web site will be up soon.

I feel like I did when I climbed up that rope in middle school. I felt a similar kind of knot in my stomach when I was halfway up, wondering if I could really do it. I feel like I'm halfway up now, and I'm struggling to inch a bit farther. "What's the move, Dan?" Look, see, move. Not look, see, stop. I have to continue to talk to people until I find the answer.

Passion is what people believe in. I need to take over the money-raising process and go after it myself. I know it can be done and that this process is for all of humanity, not just for the Latino community. We will reach thousands and thousands of people through this process and encourage sponsors to step up and take part. I want to ask them to be a part of something that will be huge—not for name value but because it is the right thing to do. I do what I do because it changes me. I look into the mirror, at a more gray man than I saw when I started this process, and I am proud of that man in the mirror. Where I once saw a little boy, and sometimes even death, I see a mature man now. I am human. With this experience has come the feeling that there is a higher cause for all of this.

I have had a lot of exposure for Imagine, and at the same time, it's been surreal because of the money situation. Still, I'm encouraged. I went to a party for a multicultural leadership foundation, and some of the biggest leaders in the Latino community were there. But I left worried about where my next meal was coming from. At the same time, I have to present myself in a way that allows people to believe in my dream. I have to act the part before I can take the part. That's a hard thing to do—a "fake it 'til you make it" kind of thing.

Staying the course means being committed to a life of excellence, not just reacting to circumstances. We all live by circumstances; everything around us is circumstances. We say, "If A happens, we'll do B. If C happens, we'll do D." We should say instead, "No matter what happens, we'll get through it." Staying the course has continued to be the anchor of my dream, the commitment to my vision. Vision is being able to open up and allow people to come in and share, not keeping it to yourself, and not believing that you are the only one that understands what you are doing.

I can't buy my son anything for Christmas. I can't even buy a tree for my home. And my bills are late. But I'm still moving forward. I know that it must be hard for any business owner who's on the verge of making it to continue pushing forward under such circumstances and building alliances. I have to keep pushing. I'm so close. This is where people fail; this is where people give up; this is when people who could have been successful say no. I have to look at things a little differently. In ninety-seven days we'll stand on that stage for the first time in Latino history, and we'll put together one of the most magnificent shows of the century.

I have had times of great excitement and a whole lot of times of great disappointment and sadness. Today I have to feel content. Who cares what happens in January? I need to focus on what's going on today. I have to step into the role of CEO. I am learning what a CEO does. I am the decision-maker. I am where the buck stops. Last night I had *tortillas* and *huevos,* something that we ate at home when I was growing up poor. It filled my stomach and it served its purpose.

December 6, 2001

We are gaining support, but even more exciting than that is the wire that went out. The Imagine 2002 press release was sent to California media, and to a newsletter for the Hispanic community nationwide. I'm excited, but I didn't know how much work would have to go into it. I've also been solidifying a relationship with my first marketing partner, the Latin Professional Network (LPN). They're going to help support the event by blasting their 6,000 members with news about Imagine.

A lot of great things are going on for me: I have contracts; I have commitments; I have a press release. But people are people, and I know that they will sometimes fail me. Or maybe I fail myself. I've got a mortgage deal that will make me $2,400. Another deal has the potential of another $8,000 or $10,000. It isn't like nothing's happening; I just have to hang on and keep working.

By contract with the Convention Center, which is the most important thing on the docket, the first rent payment is due. It looked doable at first, but then I found out that the Mastercard/Visa people won't honor the ticket sales that we are running and we won't get the money from sales that we expected to have received. I was floored when I heard. They said, "We'll pay you your money a week before the event." So I'm sitting here wondering if I have enough money to secure the Convention Center. I have enough to cover my rent, the car payment, health insurance, and child support, too. But the Convention Center is another matter.

It's all bittersweet, understanding that the pain of what I am going through will be worth it when I stand on that stage and manifest my program. Everything is about getting to that day and reaping the rewards of staying the course, staying focused, and not losing ground. I have $400 in the bank and face a crucial time ahead, and I'm nervous and very tired. My focus is on ticket sales alone. I have to pay $5,000 in bills tomorrow, and I can't help but laugh.

December 10, 2001

I renegotiated with the Convention Center to pay them on the 15th of the month! In fact, I've renegotiated everything except my rent, which I need to pay by the 5th. I'm still in the ball game! It's like climbing Mount Everest. It's a constant struggle, step by step, to make the right decisions, to make the right choices, to make the right moves. I need to step up even bigger. If we sell 300 tickets by next week, we're talking about $15,000 to $30,000. I have to utilize the tools around me. I need to convince people to help.

I need to make sure to remember to slow down and acknowledge those powerful inside conversations, thoughts, and ideas that continue to come to me throughout this process. My friend with the LPN said, "It takes a lot of guts to do what you do, Dan." I don't know that it takes a lot of guts, but it takes a lot of faith, especially in my ability to get up every morning and resume the struggle again, just to get knocked down—and then try to knock my opponent down. Usually my opponent is myself. My opponent is my guilt and my fear; my opponent is my lack of trust or lack of faith; my opponent is disbelief. Every morning it's a new opportunity to overcome obstacles. Fear, doubt, and disbelief—you gotta let it all go!

It's not the job of our friends and family to support us as much as it's our job to believe in our dream enough so that people catch the fever; that people start to walk with you. I know now from experience that there are a lot of people who do not have faith. They will not be able to stay the course, not because they're bad people, just because. Maybe it's their inability to believe in themselves. But you have to keep the spark alive. If you have a vision and you have a dream, it is your job to keep the torch burning. And when the flame gets dim, recharge and go again. Relight and reignite.

Christmas Eve, 2001

The bigger I get, the more I need; the more I need, the more money I require; the more money I require, the less I have. I can't continue to take a passive role in raising money. It's time to step up. Sometimes even the greatest intentions do not sell the vision. I've been tied up with the nuts and bolts of getting this together, but I haven't taken time to get into the real fight yet—the process of raising money.

I have to begin to look and feel like a CEO, not a little boy. It is not a little boy who is making the decisions for this corporation; it is Daniel Gutierrez, Danny Boy, Dan, all together in one, stepping up. I have to be the champion. I keep moving forward so I can prove that the American dream is still alive. We don't have to stop because our circumstances change or because one man, Osama bin Laden, decided to change our world. In fact, the very idea of that evil man gives me the energy to keep going.

I am in the process of signing a contract with the Hispanic Scholarship Fund so we can give away five scholarships to every city I go to. All my life, all I've wanted to do is to do well and to help people. Now I'm creating an event that will empower a community that has only been accustomed to working hard with its hands in order to get where it wants to go. I want to show that we Latinos can "think" our way into success. We can use our brains and talent. I want Imagine to showcase our Latino leaders. I am a motivator, and I believe in our Latino community. I will create an event that will empower others to do the same. Let's face it, people aren't going to come just to hear me—but I can offer more, I just know it.

I got a call that the motivational speaker Les Brown received my press release and wants to talk with me. I also got an e-mail from the CEO of Good Guys, asking me to go to lunch. Make the calls, Dan. Don't be scared. It's time to sell the dream. I have to renew myself and believe so that everyone else around me can, too. Never come from fear, even when a lot of crazy things are happening.

I'm less than one hundred days from creating the dream of my life. I have a feeling that these next days are going to be the most exciting days of my life—the most challenging and the most rewarding. In the midst of pulling everyone together, I need to write a speech that reflects the idea of living your dreams and passions. Financially speaking, I'm still not in a great position. But emotionally I'm feeling good. I have a negative balance of $323 in the bank, but I am absolutely powerful.

Look, see, move—the realization of a dream. We have little time for waiting or for sitting back; we must be powerful and absolutely sure in making decisions. We are creating. What excites me most is what we can create by helping each other out as Latinos, as Americans, as citizens of planet Earth. I am baffled by God's power and ability to bring things around. Accept your greatness. Step into who you are.

We have just signed on Consuelo Castillo Kickbusch, a very powerful woman in the Latino community, and a native of Laredo, Texas. Consuelo earned an ROTC commission as a second lieutenant in the U.S. Army! Our goal now is to get comic Paul Rodriguez on board.

It's interesting to be in this space today, of being okay with stillness for a few days. Christmas is here, and I've decided to take some time off until January 2nd. I'm excited about being with my baby boy, Aaron Daniel, for a week. Getting to know him even more is a blessing. I'm taking stock. A lot of great things have happened this year: My son was born, my dream was born (or at least I acted on it). Today, Christmas Eve, is a good day, a day of remembering, a day of thankfulness.

New Year's Eve, 2001
I'm listening to the song "New York, New York," and I'm thinking about September 11th. I used to listen to this song in Dallas, knowing that there was something bigger in life, that there was something to go out and get. I've spent this week with my five-month-old son, doing nothing but reading and taking care of him because he was sick. This is the year I was blessed with a son. That's the most important milestone.

What is this period in the history of our country all about? It's about freedom. It's about not allowing people to die for nothing. What is this period in my own life all about? It's about March 21, 2002, and imagining the possibilities. It's not about giving in to circumstances. It's been a great year and a hard year. It's been scary. I've cried. I've been sad, and I've been happy. Fear, I've had it; doubt, I've had it; disbelief, I've had it. Watch out, 2002, because it's going to be hot! In less than eighty days I will walk onto a stage at the Convention Center and see an ocean of people thirsty for knowledge and encouragement.

I was asked recently, "Is your fear of getting what you want bigger than your commitment to get there?" I didn't have an answer. This person said, "Well, come back when it's the opposite." I know that I am definitely committed and that this is the birth of a dream.

I am confident that we can sell these tickets. I am confident that corporate America will step up and help us make Imagine a reality. As of today, I have four speakers, not including myself: Moctesuma Esparza, the movie producer who put Jennifer Lopez on the map; Pablo Schneider, vice president and managing director of Allegiance Capital Corporation and chairman and CEO of Quantum Benefit Solutions; Christy Haubegger, the visionary founder of *Latina* magazine, the first bilingual magazine targeted exclusively at Latinas in the U.S.; and Lucia de Garcia, founder and CEO of Elan International. Twelve months to the day after I decided that I would sacrifice everything to go after this dream, people are catching the vision. This seminar will prove that anyone can do what I am doing if they just believe in themselves and accept their greatness. When we stay committed to the vision and ultimately allow people to share that vision, we can create whatever we want in our lives.

February 20, 2002

Thirty-one days until the event—thirty days if you want to count the 21st, the actual day.

To date we've had three sponsors offer a total of $7,500 for our event. It's been frustrating that even our Latino brothers and sisters have not been able to find a way to support an event that is so crucial for the community. It's almost like I'm hearing, "You can't," "You won't," and "We'll see." That's just mind-boggling. At the same time, I understand that this is my opportunity to stand up and say that it *can* be done and that there's an opportunity here for all of us to learn, including me.

I had to cut two of our speakers because we can't afford to pay them. Having to deal with egos is part of life, I guess. One woman touched my heart when she said, "Dan, don't worry about it. My ego's not that big. I support what you are doing, and I encourage you. Everybody wants to see you win." So they want to see me win, but they want me to do it on my own. Praise those people who have stepped up, even at the smallest level. Who knows how much money I've put into this myself. It's just everything I have . . . or had.

I've seen business leaders offer me $50,000 in one breath and then step away saying, "I can't give you anything." Isn't that what's reflective of our community today? We promise things we can't deliver, rather than simply saying, "I can't" or "I'm with you and I'll support you by buying a ticket." It's hard not to be bitter when people you count on say they'll support you and then they don't. It's not a Latino problem; it's a human problem. It's not just our culture that behaves this way; it's how people think in general. They don't support me because they *can't* support me; they can barely support themselves. They struggle from month to month, wondering why they can't keep their own businesses afloat. On the outside it looks great; on the inside nothing is working for them.

We're thirty-one days out. We have three sponsors, no production, and no money. Best Buy hasn't given me an answer, nor has Target. We are forced to believe in the impossible. Frankly, it's horrible. My electricity is going to be turned off any day. Nothing in my life is paid for. My child support is behind. My rent just barely got paid. I thought it would be different by now. I guess it feels that way when you're about 50 yards from the summit of Mount Everest. It seems like they should be the easiest 50 yards, but they're not. They're the most difficult. It's the last stretch before euphoria, the last stretch before it's all said and done. It's taken a lot out of me, physically, emotionally, and spiritually. I wake up every day and say, "I can. I believe I can fly. I believe I can touch the sky." Everything I know about myself I'm having to put into play right now. And for all those times when I didn't allow myself to accept my greatness, I'm accepting it today. That's all I can do on a day-to-day basis.

Thirty days. Thirty days from an event that will change lives, serve the community, realize a dream. I used to be a procrastinator, but now I'm under the gun. No more slacking and no more sleeping. I haven't even begun writing my own speech, but I know it will be about following your passion and daring to dream. Much of what

I've been through getting Imagine together will be reflected in that speech.

February 22, 2002

"Good morning! Welcome to Imagine 2002! Thank you for believing in yourselves, thank you for trusting yourselves, and most of all, thank you for supporting something that is not only way overdue, but very much needed. Accept your greatness; accept who you are. Step up into those positions."

That's what I keep thinking about saying. I have four sponsors now, all together contributing about $8,000. Then there's the reception, hosted by the Latin Business Association (LBA) and HealthNet. The reception will be outside the hall, and we'll have music and food. Everyone will be able to network after the event is over. There's nothing like empowered people networking! It's so great that the LBA is "lending" us their monthly networking event for a post-Imagine party. I can't wait to step up on that stage, regardless of what everything looks like.

Charisse Browner, the president and executive director of radio station Power 106's Knowledge Is Power Foundation, paid me a huge compliment today. She called, asking for "opinion leaders" to meet at a local high school to discuss the growing concern about African Americans and Latino Americans fighting in school. I was really honored that she had called me. When I think about it, I've been paid quite a few compliments recently. People from all over the world have called to congratulate me on having what it takes to put on this

event. A man from Argentina called me a "true visionary." Yet throughout this entire process, people have
told me "no." I have absolutely refused to give in, though,
and now I can see the finish line. It's euphoric and frustrating all at the same time. It takes sacrifice, sometimes beyond your wildest dreams, to get what you want.

The Robert Schullers and the Disneys and the Edisons
and the Gutierrezes, people who have sacrificed for their
dreams, who have been willing to put aside their own
comfort for the sake of the bigger vision, accept who
they are. They dare to be different; they dare to leave a
legacy.

Over the last few weeks, I've felt almost immobilized.
Today, though, I've gotten to feeling empowered. I believe. All the pressures of the world seem to have come
down on me at one time, which changes my perspective
in strange ways. But I'm not in despair—the pressure
has had almost a buoyant effect. My checking account
has $1.84 in it, and I have to pay tens of thousands of
dollars in twenty-nine days. It's overwhelming. I'm paying the price for that day when I can give my message of
hope and accountability to the Latino community.

I had an exciting night tonight, which is always reaf-
firming. This small-town Texas boy, little Danny, sat
next to the famous comic Paul Rodriquez. We spoke
about motivation and what our Latino community needs.
What a dream come true! I want him to present at my
program, and I'm proud to have him on my side. My
friend Manny Gonzales knows Paul's manager, and we
got together after his gig at the Grove in Anaheim. It
was surreal being asked to step into his dressing room.

He asked me, "So you want me to do what? Be funny?" I said, "No, Paul. I want you to be real. Life hasn't always been funny for you, right?" Then he cleared the room and began to tell me his story. Turns out I was right. "That's what people want to hear, Paul," I told him. "They can identify with the man as well as the movie star." It was fascinating to hear him talk about how tough things are. He understands struggle. It left a huge impression on me, and I knew it was a big career step for me. Sitting there in his room made me realize how real this whole process is.

I also ran into Mark Victor Hansen, the man who co-authored *Chicken Soup for the Soul*. I shook his hand and gave him my business card. Who knows? All these folks will know who I am in due time. It's 11:30 at night, and I don't need to go home and go straight to bed just to toss and turn and worry. I need to live my life, something I've had trouble with. Ironically, I've been so stuck in creating passion I've forgotten who I am and where I'm going. It was a great day, though, and there are more to come.

March 1, 2002
We're three weeks away! I'm scared to death. We're still not selling enough tickets. My stomach hurts and I'm not sleeping well. So much work needs to be done, I'm very concerned. I can see success, taste success, but I'm a bundle of nerves. I caught myself saying, "Do I really want to go there? Should I bail out now?" I don't even know what to do with the credit card numbers people have used to pay for their tickets. I'm not ap-

proved yet! Finding these kind of solutions is difficult for me right now. We can still sell this event out, but I have to believe it before anybody else will. I haven't felt a knot in my stomach like this in a long time. It's caused by utter ignorance of what's next.

Everybody's sending out e-mails, but there's got to be another way to get people to buy tickets. I can't lower the price. I dreamed last night that I was standing in front of a brick wall. Twenty-one days out. Maybe my focus should be on renegotiating everything again. Maybe that's the route. Maybe we should drop payments again. I just don't know.

March 4, 2002

Things aren't much different than they were a few days ago . . . when everything was falling apart. There isn't enough money, as of today, to make this project work. But I'm taking the approach that Imagine will go on. We'll have fun whether it's two hundred, five hundred, or a thousand people. My job is to cut costs to the point where we can afford to do anything at all. I'm asking speakers to speak for free. I'm getting my production down to almost nothing. I may not even have anything but audio and video available, so people will have to hear the message without the glamor. Ironically, I woke up this morning feeling really empowered. I'm going to keep preparing, start writing my speech, and I'm just going to believe that people will come.

Nothing has turned out the way I saw it in the beginning. Corporate America has not stepped up the way I expected, and who's to say it's their job to do so in the first place? One thing I do know is that people are excited about Imagine. People are looking forward to being part of something that's historic. I think that some people just want to see if I can go through with it. Various business groups have shown interest, but they have yet to buy tickets. My job is to put it on, to see it through, to not be scared, even though I am. What's wrong with being scared? After all, that's when the paralysis stops and I move forward. It's been a long and powerful lesson. Everything is still possible. Things don't look good right now, but that's just a state of being. I need to keep pushing.

This could potentially be the time when I give up and say, "Why me? Why do I have to go through so much?" Yet everything in me, everything I believe in, says, "Stay the course, Dan. The winds are high; the surf is rough. Your tiny ship is beaten and battered. But continue moving forward. Don't give up." That's what I have to hang on to. This is my journey, and it's my responsibility to get to the end of it.

It's March 4th, and I'm still looking for solutions. I'm looking for the "how to's," not the "if's"; I'm looking for the ways to make it happen. I'm right at the place where I need to step it up even more. I feel almost euphoric. I'm on the final stretch on that rope again, and I feel exactly the same way—with a knot in my stomach, wondering how I'll do it. Can I keep this beaten, battered ship afloat and get it to the harbor, where we can rest?

March 14, 2002

I'm ready to start writing my speech. Is everything still falling apart? Yes. I'm holding this ship together with one nail. Yesterday I was at the point of meltdown. I ended up going home midafternoon and just unplugged. Any time you are in a dangerous zone of passion, I think there's a need to stop and do nothing for a day. Things were looking hopeless, so I came home and did nothing. A friend of mine came over and we talked. We agreed that sometimes we need to let go of things—let go and let God, as the old saying goes. If you let go, things come back. My speaking coach once told me that I needed to sit at the pool for a week. I remember laughing and saying, "A week I'm going to sit at the pool? I need to make money!" It was a struggle, but the truth is that everything became more clear after some rest. I could think about solutions. That's what has happened in these past couple of days. Today I stayed at home and did nothing until 1:00. When I got back to work, things were somehow less daunting.

Maybe I'm trying too hard. Maybe it's time for me to allow everyone else to do their job—to sell tickets. I can get on the phone and encourage people to step up, to show up, and to support this event. We've sold two hundred tickets. We need to sell a thousand to break even. I just don't know.

March 19, 2002

Best Buy has committed $20,000 as a charter sponsor!

I got a call from another potential sponsor, a credit card company: "We're trying to work things out for you."

All of a sudden things aren't quite as bad as they'd seemed. I also did an interview over the phone for Latinola.com.

In the past few days everything has changed. It's a pivotal point: If you believe in what you are doing for long enough, people will catch the fever, even at the last hour. I gave six years of my life to Best Buy, and now they're honoring me by supporting an event that will promote diversity within their company and the community. And they're supporting me. Time to move, time to groove; time to look for solutions and continue pushing and believing in the possibilities.

Tomorrow will be a very difficult day.

No! It's not going to be a difficult day! In any case, we must raise $5,000 to $7,000 so that we can continue on. I spoke to Hugo Enciso, in the business marketing department of *La Opinion*, about my upcoming ad. Tomorrow really will be the last push for us. We'll always be wavering financially, but after this business is over I will begin to connect spiritually with myself and the task ahead. I honestly believe that Imagine will change lives.

I had a wonderful breakfast with Moctesuma this morning to discuss getting these last days out of the way. I feel at peace today. I'm at the five yard line. I am not stressed, and I have begun to let go and let fate take over. Right on, right on.

Mere days from today we'll be creating history with Imagine 2002. I'm very tired, exhausted in every way—emotionally, physically, mentally—but I'm happy to be part of something so big. I'll pick up my son this afternoon. I'm excited about that because when he's around, my world seems just to revolve around serving him! My legs are weak; my spirit, although high, is tired. All I can think about is the finish line, just making it across that finish line.

Yesterday I spent the day at the Convention Center with the film crew, the production crew, the stage manager, and my logistics team. We walked and talked through the day. I loved the cameras, and I can't wait to see the end result. When I think about all the hard work that has gone into this, I can't help but think about all of the people out there who want something big out of their own lives. Aspiring entertainers, students, retirees, housewives, blue collar workers, sons and daughters of the prestigious: Stay committed to your dream.

Your past is not who you are. Your past is only a springboard, an opportunity to compare and contrast, to do something different, to see through someone else's eyes. The past is a tool we all need to build up, not tear down.

I can proudly say that I haven't sabotaged anything. I believe and see big things and I accept them. I embrace them! I'm focused on seeing it through, finishing the race, feeling the pain. I've had an opportunity now to believe it, to feel it, to accept it, to conquer it. Imagine 2002, here we come!

Chapter 8

The Agony and the Ecstasy of Living Your Dreams

*My job was to get to this day. You see empty
seats. I see opportunity.*

• • • • • • • • • • •

"Tomorrow is the day," I thought to myself on March 20,
2002. I had been up all night preparing logistics. Because of budget shortfalls, I had very little help in getting the details completed. I finally crashed at about
two o'clock A.M. I was exhausted and I needed to get
some rest—I was due at the Convention Center at six
A.M. My dear friend Diane had secretly showered my hotel
room at the Figueroa in downtown Los Angeles with
candles and flowers so that I could get my mind in the
right place for my big day. After tossing and turning, I
finally fell asleep, only to succumb to very vivid dreams
of what the coming day would bring.

In the morning, the first thing I noticed was that I
was very sick. My throat felt like I had been swallowing
nails all night, and I had a fever. All the stress had finally gotten to me, and my body was screaming for help.
I started crying. How could this happen to me at the

last minute? How would I be able to emcee the event
and then be the last speaker of the day? Would I have it
in me to get the job done? I had learned by then that
most people don't concern themselves about other
people's personal problems. They have their own, after
all. They had paid to see an event, and it was my job to
give it to them. I decided not to let anyone know just
how sick I was.

Then, like the true warrior I was, I got out of bed, I
opened the window, and I looked out onto the city. I
could see the sun coming up over the skyline. I immediately reached over and grabbed my CD player and a
disk that had been a strong source of inspiration for
me: "I Believe I Can Fly" by James Ingram. I had heard
him sing his rendition at the Crystal Cathedral and had
made it my theme song. There I sat, feeling like an eigh-
teen-wheeler had just run over me, and I began the song.
I turned it up as loud as I could stand it, and I stood in
front of the open shutters of my fifteenth-floor hotel room,
belting out the lyrics with everything I had. I sang to the
world.

> I used to think that I could not go on,
> That life was nothing but an awful song,
> But now I know the meaning of true love.
> I'm leaning on the everlasting arms.
>
> If I can see it, then I can do it.
> If I just believe it, there's nothing to it.
>
> I believe I can fly.
> I believe I can touch the sky.
> I think about it every night and day,
> Spread my wings and fly away.
> I believe I can soar.

I see me running through that open door.
I believe I can fly, I believe I can fly, I believe I can fly.

See, I was on the verge of breaking out.
Sometimes silence can seem so loud.
There are miracles in life I must achieve,
But first I know it starts inside of me.

If I can see it, then I can do it.
If I just believe it, there's nothing to it.

I believe I can fly.
I believe I can touch the sky.
I think about it every night and day,
Spread my wings and fly away.
I believe I can soar.
I see me running through that open door.
I believe I can fly, I believe I can fly, I believe I can fly,
'Cause I believe in you.

If I can see it, then I can be it.
If I just believe it, there's nothing to it.

I believe I can fly.
I believe I can touch the sky.
I think about it every night and day,
Spread my wings and fly away.
I believe I can soar.
I see me running through that open door.
I believe I can fly, I believe I can fly, I believe I can fly.

All of a sudden, everything I had been through—all of
my life—was right in front of me. This was my day to
shine. It was my day to fly. I wasn't about to let anything tell me differently. The belief that I had formed as
a young man that I was a failure was fading into the
distant past; the drugs that had kept me chained as a
young man in my twenties were unlocked, and I was
standing tall and strong. I must have played the song at
least ten times. As people walked by on the sidewalk
below, they must have thought a madman had finally

lost it. But through those words I was accepting my greatness—I was stepping into it. Success was up to me. Take no prisoners. Burn the bridge behind me. There had been opportunities for retreat, but now it was do or die, and I was ready to do!

I got everything together and headed over to the Convention Center. I had forgotten that I was sick. Producing this event was more important than anything else I had on my mind, including my health. I arrived around dawn and looked out at the huge room with a thousand empty chairs waiting to be filled. We had, at best, three hundred registrations, but I was hopeful that the advertising we had done in *La Opinion* and *The Excelsior* in Orange County would drive the numbers in. I was about to learn some big lessons about putting on events: Never count on ticket sales to make or break you.

I had been previously scheduled to do interviews with the *Los Angeles Times*, the *Orange County Register,* and *La Opinion.* They kept asking, "Where are all the people? Is the Latino community ready for empowerment?" I was not used to this kind of badgering from the media, but I answered their questions the best I could: "My job has been to get to this day and to prove that anyone can fulfill their dreams if they want it badly enough. You see empty seats, whereas I see opportunity. Our community must begin to come together. We must learn to help each other and mentor each other to greatness."

With that, I walked out onto the stage and began Imagine 2002. One by one, Paul Rodriguez, Christie Haubegger, Moctesuma Esparza, Lucia de Garcia, Pablo Schneider, and Consuelo Castillo–Kickbusch stepped up and delivered their messages. I couldn't have been prouder of their performances. They spoke to the few that were there as if they were a crowd of 100,000, and they encouraged everyone to bring more people next year.

With things progressing smoothly on stage, I allowed myself to feel some of the stress of not having enough attendance. It meant that there wouldn't be enough funds to pay all of the expenses incurred. During the lunch break, Monica, my son's mother, came to offer me lunch. We shared it in the green room, and at one point she looked at me intensely and asked, "Dan, are you sick?" No one had been able to see that I was in pain—I was doing a great job of hiding it—but Monica knew me better than anyone there. With some hesitation, I told her that I had a fever and that my throat hurt badly. It lent some momentary comfort that I could acknowledge my mental and physical state, but I assured her (and myself) that I wouldn't let anything distract me from my goal, which at that point was to finish the event.

I must admit, I was beginning to feel somewhat defeated. How would I tell my people that I wouldn't be able to pay all of the expenses? Then, when Moctesuma began to speak, I listened. He said that everyone has a story. So what? That was all I needed to hear. This audience had come to hear me speak, and, as they say in Hollywood, "The show must go on!"

As Moctesuma wrapped up, I got ready to do what I had dreamed of for years. Although I had some powerful speakers with me, I was the producer, the emcee, the final speaker, and the visionary behind Imagine. I

was the center of attention. I consciously devoted myself to stepping into my greatness, and I stepped up to
the mic and began. My voice was raspy and hoarse, but
I ignored it.

> We must all learn to accept our greatness. At one
> point or another, all of these speakers, and all suc-
> cessful people, have had to look at themselves in the
> mirror and be happy with what they see. That means
> looking into your own eyes and seeing the very soul
> of who you were designed to be. Not a taller, smarter,
> better-looking, better-built you. You: just the way
> you are.
>
> I can remember fourteen months ago looking deep
> into my own eyes and saying, "Dan, you have what it
> takes just the way you are. We were all created for
> greatness from the very start. Things like fear, doubt,
> and disbelief change our perceptions of what could
> be true, and so we settle and quit trying! We allow
> our past to dictate our future, rather than our future
> being run by the desire to use the past as a stepping-
> stone.
>
> Accepting your greatness is also about accepting
> the greatness in others and in the Latino community,
> and assisting other Latinos to get to higher places. It
> means not closing the door behind you and saying, "I
> got mine, now you get yours."
>
> If we want to see change in the statistics, we here
> in this room have to start now. We have to accept the
> greatness within us. Look at the person sitting next
> to you and tell them, "I accept my greatness and I
> accept your greatness." Do it now! Whatever position
> you have in your company, reach to the next posi-
> tion. Reach to that boardroom and don't be told you
> can't! If you see a brown ceiling, quit looking at it, or
> paint it another color. It will continue to exist as long
> as you acknowledge it!
>
> Accepting your greatness is about self-account-
> ability—taking personal accountability for the way
> you choose to live your life!

Live your dreams and your passions. What is your passion? Your passion is that thing that nags at you and won't go away. It's that thing that, in a perfect world, you would do. It's that thing that, if given a choice in life, you would do it for free, or maybe you already do. It's that dream that you have the greatest fear about, because the fear of failing is greater, and so you stay comfortable and live a life of mediocrity.

I remember thinking to myself about today: Will anyone come? Does anyone care? What if no one cares what I have to say? Your passion is that dream that you were all put on this earth to do. That one thing that, when your life is over, you can say, "I did it!"

Les Brown asks a question in his seminars: Where is the richest soil in the world? No, it's not the Middle East with their oil. No, it's not Africa with their diamond mines. My friends, the richest soil on earth is in your local cemetery. Yes, folks, there in your local cemetery lies all the wealth in the world. You see, there are all the incomes of all the doctors, lawyers, astronauts, mothers, and fathers that could have been. You see, they went to their graves with dreams unfulfilled.

I remember September 11th like it was yesterday. I remember turning on the TV and being in shock about what had happened. As the death toll rose, I couldn't help but think about all those lives that had just vanished into thin air. I could see a mom or dad, a child, a brother or sister, a girlfriend or boyfriend. If anything, we should be walking memorials for all the people who died that day, and for all the men and women who are fighting our war so that we can live our passions and dreams. I refuse to let that happen. I have proven to the world that the American Dream is alive and well, and we can still live life to its fullest! So look for the signs that are around you that say, "Yes, you are on the right track. Keep going!"

I remember at the beginning of this project I wondered if I was doing the right thing. Should I do it, or should I give up? I was so confused that I just cried out, "Why can't this idea just leave my head!?" Then I reminded myself, "Stay the course, stay focused."

The most important message I can tell you today is to focus. Live a life of commitment. Be committed to the outcome, no matter what! Never allow circumstances to dictate outcomes. You can bet that there will be storms, because as soon as you tell someone that you are chasing your passion, people will come out of nowhere to tell you that you can't. Everything that might go wrong can go wrong. The storms can get so heavy that you will want to quit. There have been several times during this journey when I wanted to stop. Many times when I lost focus and walked down the wrong path I would ask myself, "Dan, are your actions at this moment in direct alignment with your dreams and goals?"

I live with a minute-by-minute redirection of my motives. Sometimes I have literally cried all the way home, wondering, "What do I do next?" On the worst day of my life—or at least I thought it was—I remember being ready to head out the door and conquer the world. Little did I know that that day would be a test of my commitment to my dream. When I woke up, I received a call from the finance company for my car. I was told that they were going to repossess it. I thought, "Oh well, I'll take care of it today." Then I brushed it off and headed out the door, only to find a notice on the door from my landlord telling me to pay up or move out.

I had just deposited some money in the bank. I got to work and balanced my checkbook, but then found out that one of the checks I deposited had bounced. I had a negative balance of $283.15. I thought to myself, "THIS IS THE WORST DAY OF MY LIFE!" I put my head down on my desk and yelled out to God, "If this is the way that living a dream is supposed to be, I'd rather not be alive." I decided at that moment that I would drive home and hide. I had $1.00 to my name. At least I could go to Jack-in-the-Box and get two tacos for 99 cents.

When I got to the fast food restaurant, something
happened that would change my life. I was pulling
up to the drive-through line when, all of a sudden,
two men in a black Mercedes convertible began to
argue. The fight escalated, and like a slow motion
movie, one of them cried out for help. I was in New-
port Beach, one of the most expensive places to live
in America. "Maybe this was part of a movie?" I
thought. I looked around for cameras, but there
weren't any. This was for real!

I was only about 20 yards from the men, and I
could clearly hear one of them yelling, "Please help
me! He's trying to kill me!" I could see then that they
were fighting over a gun, and I watched in horror as
the gun went off. One of the men then stood up,
pointed the gun at the other man's chest, and fired,
then fired again at his head. The man fell back in the
seat. I could see he was dead, and I sat there wondering if this madman with the gun would shoot
me next. Instead, he very casually put his weapon
on the trunk of the Mercedes and lit a cigarette. It
was all over in a matter of minutes. Soon there were
police everywhere. I stood as still as a statue for
fear that the cops would think I was part of the
crime.

Within minutes, about six people who had witnessed the event, including me, were whisked away
to the police station so that the media could not get
to us. We were not allowed to share anything that
pertained to the murder with each other, so we
began to ask each other what we did for a living. One
woman finally looked at me and asked me the same
question. I said, "I'm a motivator." They all responded in unison, "Then motivate us!" I smiled and
said, "Okay, I will."

I began to tell them the story of my day. When I
got to the end, I said, "You see, this morning I cried
to God that I didn't want to live my dreams and
passions. It was too hard. Then I heard a man cry for
his life, and then he was dead. I was the last person
to hear his plea. He no longer has his children, his

family, no one. It can be that fast for all of us, and we must remember this day." I looked at each of them in the eye. "It could have been any of us."

That day gave me a new perspective on life. I needed to be grateful for what I had, and I knew that God would be faithful in his time. I had a dream and a choice to carry on. I did just that.

Staying the course is about sacrifice. You have to be willing to sacrifice all you have for what you believe in. You will never know how far you can go until you have gone too far, and at that point, my friends, you have already become complacent. Keep on pushing!

I was terribly relieved to be at the end of my speech. Then, to my shock and surprise, all two hundred people took to their feet and gave me a standing ovation. All my work, all my anguish, all my sleepless nights, my sore throat, and my 103 degree fever were forgotten in the moment. I was being honored for my work, and that was the greatest reward I think I'd ever received!

· · · · · · · · · · ·

The next morning I went to the pool to relax and think. "What now?" was my overriding thought. I had spent all of a year working day and night to create a dream. The *Orange County Register* business section reported in big headlines that morning: "Forum Turnout Low." There was an accompanying photo of Paul Rodriquez and me. I was quoted as saying, "I'd be remiss to say I'm not disappointed." It had been a long year of ups and downs. To go through with it or not had been the recurrent question for me over the past year.

THE AGONY AND THE ECSTASY

One thing was true, though. I had done what I said I would do. I had produced an event. Another article on Latinola.com, by Manny Gonzales, stated:

> Los Angeles has been the nation's largest Latino city for some time now, but it seems there is still plenty of opportunity to make history. On March 21, 2002, Los Angeles will play host to Imagine 2002, the first-ever motivational speakers' forum targeting U.S. Latinos. But before there was ever any talk about this highly anticipated event for Latinos, there was a dream: Daniel Gutierrez's dream, that is.

There were many lessons I had learned, and many more that I would still learn. In the end, though, I had done what I had set out to do, and there was a great sense of pride that went with that. The people who attended the event, all two hundred of them, had gotten something out of it, as had the speakers. I got a slew of letters and e-mails in the following days:

> As a Hispanic woman entrepreneur, I truly believe the importance of gathering our strengths, our lives, and our professional experiences so that we can leverage our GREATNESS and become stronger, individually and as a community. Again, I thank you for making this happen.
> —Adriana Eiriz, CEO, Latin Links, Inc.

> I just wanted to take an opportunity to tell you what an awesome experience I had at your Imagine 2002: 1st Annual Latino Motivational Seminar, yesterday. I was so high all day long; I met so many awesome people at every break. My friend and I were full of emotions all day, rejoicing for your tremendous achievement and feeling your pain in the turnout. However, I believe in quality, not quantity, and if you affected just one person, it was worth it. I am here to

say you profoundly affected my life. I really felt as if
my own purpose and vision was clarified. I even re-
wrote my company mission statement and revised
my tag line when I got home. I had a wonderful session with my coaching client using the tools learned
during the seminar.
—Deborah Cujiño-Deras, M.S., C.R.C.

I wanted to take this opportunity to thank you for
putting on such a life-changing presentation. The
speakers were excellent, and they all coincide on how
I feel with regards to my life goals and past experiences. I honestly believe that we Latinos need to help
each other out in a collaborated effort to achieve
individual and community goals and objectives. I
thank you because now I know that there are more
individuals than myself that share the same vision.
Many Latinos say they want change, but few are
willing to do something about it. And we, such as
those in attendance, are a minority within a minority
that are taking that forward step to make things
happen.
—Esteban Cota

I want to thank you dearly for the wonderful event
you put on last Thursday—for (in your words) "accepting your greatness," and forging forward to what
you believe to be true. This conference needed to
take place and you did it . . . for that I congratulate
you. The speakers were phenomenal and were right
on the mark. Although I thought I already knew
some of these things (go figure), I need to hear them
again, and again, and again, from a fresh perspective. I left the Convention Center feeling even more
inspired and motivated to continue along my journey, and with great hope for our community. I feel in
my heart of hearts that every person that needed to
be there to hear the message was there . . . not one
person more, not one person less. I feel my attendance at this conference was a call to action to bring
this type of information to our community. Like I

THE AGONY AND THE ECSTASY

mentioned to you at the conference, I've made a personal commitment to bring at least 10 people with me next year. As I was sitting there, I was thinking how it would have benefited my best friend to have been sitting there listening, how it would have benefited my brother, my sister, my co-workers, etc. . . . and in that moment I made the commitment to myself to bring them along next year (your job, should you choose to accept it, is to make next year's conference as great, or even better, than this year's). Oh!, and by the way, I got some business while I was at it, too!

Your story about the day that changed your life touched me and reminded me of my own "day that changed my life." I, too, made a dramatic change in careers to follow my heart and to live my passion. It is encouraging to see more and more people doing the same. It takes courage and a lot of faith in the process of life. The more of us who are out there sharing our stories, the more we will inspire others to do the same. It feels great to be a part of the shift that is taking place right now.

Once again, thank you for being that pioneer our community so desperately needed. If you need any support in any way, please know that you can count on me. I believe in what "accepting your greatness" is all about, and would like to support you in taking that to the Latino community.
—Ximena Salazar, Feng Shui Essentials

It was a great conference! It was both a cultural experience to me and a personal challenge regarding what to do with my private practice.
—Steve Meyer, Ph.D.

I have attended many events at which I met and listened to Og Mandino, Anthony Robbins, Zig Ziglar, Jack Canfield, and Mark Victor Hansen. I can honestly say that the line-up of speakers presented at *Imagine 2002* ranks among the very best.
—Esteban G. Gallegos, attorney at law

I was glowing. A small-town boy from Midlothian, Texas, had just made his mark on a city as big as Los Angeles. Now I was ready for the world. It was true that anyone could have their dream if they wanted it badly enough, and I had just proved it. I took a simple idea—a thought—and I had turned it into a reality.

I couldn't have done it without my great sponsors, and gratefully acknowledge HealthNet of California, the Hispanic Chamber of Orange County, Profiles International, Hollywood.com, Aramark, LatinoLA, State Farm, Turn it Digital, *La Opinion,* Solomon Smith Barney, Latin Business Association, LPN, Countrywide, U.S. Hispanic Contractors Association, National Association of Hispanic Professionals, and the Best Buy Company—my founding partner. It had been four years since I had left Best Buy and decided to chase my dreams. It was a testament to their honor that they were my presenting sponsor for this event. All these companies had believed in my vision when I had been told that I would never get a dime. Sapo Communications, to this day, still believes in my mission, and their patience has allowed me to continue to grow.

There were also many individuals who helped to make Imagine 2002 a success. Without them, I could not have succeeded. Pablo Schneider, Moctesuma Esparza, Paul Rodriguez, Consuelo Kichbusch, Joe Conway, Lacy Hildago, Trent Esperti, Rick Gilliam, Jim Ort, Sande Herron, Kat Ohlman, Monica Cousins, and the many, many friends and supporters who continue to support my dream and vision give me ultimate hope and confidence.

Even with all this support, though, we had failed to raise enough money to cover the huge expenses we had incurred, mostly because of my inexperience in the event business. Now it was time to face reality. The event was now over, and it all seemed very anticlimactic. I was proud of my accomplishments, but now it was time to look at the bottom line. I had believed all along that with the vendors and speakers we would raise the necessary funds. The truth was, even with great sponsors, we were about $95,000 short of making Imagine a profitable event. I looked at that number and thought it may as well have been $1,000,000. I had no feasible way to meet my commitments.

It took me a while to realize that I needed to keep on moving and working as a speaker, though, and I was committed to making sure that every vendor and speaker was paid for their part in the event. To this day, I am still paying off the debt from Imagine 2002.

I struggled with the idea of doing it all over again. And then that little voice in my head said, "Daniel, create another event. The worst thing you can do is stop now."

This time I would have some help from a good friend, Mike Aguilera, of San Jose, California. Mike had called me several times asking if I would stage an Imagine event in San Jose. After much convincing, I decided to go for it. San Jose ended up being a huge success by all my standards: We filled the 400-seat auditorium with 350 people, and the media loved it. The headline in the *Observador* the day after the event read "Hundreds Attend Motivational Forum!" What a difference! I was over the moon. As of late 2003, we have returned to Los Angeles for a second event, and we created a new and successful Inagine event in Dallas.

Dreaming is about taking risks; it's going against the grain and being willing to take the overwhelming waves of criticism that come out of being a visionary. It's about looking for validation from within and not from others. It's about trusting your God and knowing that you will be victorious. It's about stepping into your greatness and believing in yourself and your dream until the whole world does, too. My dream for the next event is a sold-out Staples Center in downtown Los Angeles. I see Carlos Santana playing to a crowd of 20,000, and then me delivering a message of hope and empowerment to the attendees. Do you see it? I do!

PART THREE

STEPPING INTO
YOUR
GREATNESS

Chapter 9

Success Is Believing in What You Cannot See

Remember, reaching your dreams is about having faith that what you are holding true in your mind will manifest itself, even when current appearances tell you otherwise.

• • • • • • • • • • •

When I took on the project of creating a Latino success forum, I had a very clear picture in my mind of what I wanted it to look like. By March 21, 2002, I had seen the whole event, every detail, in my mind a thousand times. I had imagined exactly what it would look like. I even had a good idea of what it would feel like. As a matter of fact, very little of my vision turned out to be true. I had seen at least 1,000 people in attendance, along with a huge after-party. In reality, there were between 150 and 200 people that day. The stage hadn't been as glamorous as I had wanted, but at least there had been a stage. There were no fancy lights, but there was lighting. In all, the most important things there were the speakers and myself. I had, in fact, made it!

In order to achieve something, you must first be able to see it in your mind's eye. Furthermore, if you have any doubts that you can achieve what you want, you will fail. If you think about it, you make decisions every single day that are based on whether or not you *think* you can do it, even if it's just crossing the street! The opposite is true as well. If you are certain that you will meet with success, you will try anything! You will always prove yourself right, whether it's negative or positive. Whatever it is that you choose to believe in, despite what may seem to be true according to appearances, it will always manifest itself. You always have the power to choose results. It's all in your mind and based on your faith. The funny thing about results is, you're going to get them no matter what you do, so why not go for results that reflect your goals and aspirations?

· · · · · · · · · · ·

I am asked to speak to many young people, and I find that they usually teach me as much as I teach them. A few years back, I was asked to talk with a class of Latino students at a high school in East L.A. I was there to share the idea of visualizing dreams with them, down to the very last detail. I asked for a volunteer to help make my point. A young lady raised her hand and was brave enough to play along with me. In front of the class, I asked her to close her eyes and concentrate. A chorus of giggles rose and then fell. Everyone recognizes how hard it is to act as the proverbial guinea pig.

After the kids quieted down, I asked her the first question: "Luisa, what do you want to do after you graduate?"

"I want to be an interior designer," she answered immediately. I was secretly very pleased with her answer—

I related to it very much. Another round of laughs took over the room.

I smiled. "Great!" I said. "So, Luisa, tell me, what kind of car does an interior designer drive?"

Again, she answered right away. "A BMW!" Luisa was brave; she didn't mind the teasing by her classmates at all.

"Great," I said. "What does the BMW look like?"

Now she laughed herself. "It's shiny and red, like a fire engine."

Now I was going to start to really get her thinking. I scratched my chin and looked right into her eyes. "Luisa, what color is the dashboard light?"

That one wasn't so easy, but it didn't take long before she answered, "I want it to be red, too."

"Where do you live when you're an interior designer?"

I could tell she was starting to get into this exercise. She took a little more time to answer now, giving it some thought.

"I think I would live in the Fairfax district, close to the museum. I really like it there. I'd live in one of those 1930s houses with a big lawn in front."

I asked her more questions about what various aspects of her life would be like. I didn't particularly focus on marriage or relationships. I wanted to motivate her to move forward. Of course, I had to finally ask, "Luisa, do you know what an interior designer makes?"

She knew the answer. "About $75,000, after training!"

It was doable. Her life would no doubt take many turns. All lives do. But I wanted to instill in her a reason to live a life of moving forward, of acting, because she saw a dream in her mind's eye, and she wouldn't let it go. The dream might evolve and change over time, but she would have set a goal for herself—and she could actually see every little detail, down to a dashboard light.

There was one last question. "What are you doing right now, outside of school, to make that dream come true? Are you acting on it? Are you seeking out other interior designers to talk with and get advice from?"

Now Luisa's grin turned south. She had to admit that she hadn't gone that far yet. I reminded her that she was young and she had plenty of time, but it could never hurt to get out and actively follow her dreams and learn more about them. What I didn't say aloud was that Luisa was probably from a very poor home. I was proud that she hadn't let that get in the way. She clearly already had the desire to do better.

Luisa chased me down after class and thanked me for the exercise. She said to me, "Mr. Gutierrez, can I really be an interior designer? My dad says I can't, and as much as I love him, he frustrates me every day." My heart sank as I heard the desperate plea of this young woman.

"Luisa," I said, "never let anyone decide for you what you can or can't be. Always respect your mother and father, and understand that they are just trying to protect you from harm. But if you keep dreaming and believing in the things you told me in class, you will reach any dream you set your heart and mind to achieve." I completely understood where she was coming from. In my house growing up, it was my stepfather who had dampened my dreams when I expressed them.

I hadn't been much older than Luisa when I'd picked up the Yellow Pages and called every interior designer in the book, literally. My resolve back then had been so strong because I had developed a picture of what I wanted. I'd always had a vivid imagination. I was always running, but sometimes I actually ran in the right direction, toward a better life. I had created an indelible image of the future, no matter what my goal was at the time.

I also realized early on that image is, in fact, important. That may not be a politically correct thing to say, but I believe it's true. I honestly believe that my attention to fashion had allowed me opportunities I wouldn't otherwise have had. Something deep inside had motivated me when I'd walked into Trammell Crowe's office, or when I'd been able to get into the diamond district. I had dressed for success.

When I first started in the business world, I'd looked at magazines for guidance, and to this day, I still look at what people are wearing, and then I jazz it up a bit. I may not have been able to get where I'd gone in a pair of sweats. Even in high school, I dressed up most of the time. I always felt that it was important to leave the house looking like a million bucks. You never know who you are going to run into. Along with dress, the ability to carry yourself like you are important is crucial. I remember walking into a hospital once. The nurse at the front desk had said, "Doctor, what floor are you visiting

today?" I responded very naturally, "The fourth, please."
She then asked one more question that perhaps gave
me away. "Doctor, what is your name so that I can sign
you in?" "Doctor Love," I responded with a flash of a
smile.

When I'd been managing Best Buy, employees would
tell me daily that they thought they should be promoted.
Everyone wanted to be a supervisor. Even back then, I'd
tell them that they needed to look like managers before
becoming managers. That's just the way it is.

Opening Yourself to the Possibilities

What aspirations do you have? The two exercises in this
chapter will help you to open yourself up to the possibilities. They're fun and they're easy to do. Find a place
where you can be alone, and when you do them, above
all else, be honest!

EXERCISE: VISUALIZATION

Life happens through a series of days, but the future
keeps you going, and the more you can emulate your
dream image, the more likely it is to come to fruition.
We spend time all through the week thinking about
plans for the weekend. Now it's time to make plans for
the future. Let your imagination run wild here.

If you could be anyone in this world, who would you
want to be? _____

_____

What does that person do? _____

_____

_____

What kind of income does that person make? _____

_____

What kind of car does this person drive?_____

_____

Describe the car down to the littlest details: color, type
of tires, interior, and so on._____

_____

_____

_____

What kind of social status does this person have? And
are they a leader or a follower?_____

_____

_____

_____

Where does this person dine?_____

_____

_____

Does this person have a family?_____

_____

_____

_____

What does this person wear? Are they casual? Do they dress in business attire? Describe him or her all the way down to the smallest detail: cufflinks for the men, the type of purse for the ladies._____

_____

_____

_____

_____

_____

_____

After you have finished answering these questions, take a moment to actually visualize yourself. Create a mental image. Watch yourself. Picture waking up in the morning and looking at your surroundings. Dress yourself and take care with the details. When you take your dream car out to your dream job, smell the interior. Imagine a day in the life of your future self.

Now, when you stand up, let all of those dreams stream through your body. Feel them in your muscles, your bones, your heart. How do you hold your head now? How do you walk? How do you carry yourself now that you know what your dreams are? The most magical thing is, you *are* that person already! You have work to do, but everything you need is right there with you. It feels awkward to change styles, to alter the way you dress or speak or behave. You can't do it in a day or a week or even a year. But every day, you must carry that image of yourself—the person you want to be. Eventually, you will be able to step into your greatness.

• • • • • • • • • •

Remember to dream of tomorrow, but walk in today.

• • • • • • • • • •

EXERCISE: THE DREAM BOARD

Even during my lowest periods, I always retained a
spark of hope. During the good times, it roared like
fire. When I was at my wit's end, my dreams were the
only thing that kept me going. I would remember Paris
and St. Peter's Cathedral in Rome. I would remember
the Emmys and turning a losing store into a very
profitable one. I would remember flying to Mexico on a
private plane and the ocean view from the hills of
Laguna Beach.

At a certain point, probably some afternoon while I
was out of work, wondering what I was going to do,
with my brain scattered in a thousand directions, I got
creative. I made what I would later call my Dream
Board. It has been one of the most effective tools I
have used in achieving my dreams. Dream Boarding
sounds like something a surfer would do, and in a
way, that is what you're doing. Instead of riding a
wave, though, you are riding your dreams. And the
board reminds you on a daily basis of what you really
want. It allows you to connect to a vision bigger than
yourself in the here and now. It inspires you to stay
focused, and it serves as motivation on those frequent
days when you really don't want to push through the
problems of daily life.

Now I keep my Dream Board right in front of me in my office. I haven't always had it so near, and it has seen the inside of a closet, but I use it now more than ever because it gives me so much encouragement. Where you keep your Dream Board is entirely up to you. It belongs to you, and you can do whatever you want with it, to it, or about it. Don't worry what anyone will think about you creating this tool. Your family might tease you, but set your pride aside. If you ever think of your Dream Board as something to be ashamed of, you will put your dreams in great jeopardy.

These are the supplies you'll need:

- A pair of scissors
- A glue stick
- A piece of foam or poster board at least a half-inch thick. The size is up to you. I use a full poster-size board.
- A frame that you can put the board in when you are finished
- A variety of magazines and newspapers. Try to get at least ten, or more if you can. It's important that you have different types of magazines. They don't specifically have to be magazines you normally read, but they should reflect some of your interests. The images inside are what's important.
- Your dreams and aspirations. This is the most important ingredient! You also need to be willing to work with your ego.

The Dream Board is just what it sounds like. Your job is to page through magazines, and when you see something that inspires you, whatever it might be, you'll cut out the picture and glue it to the poster board. You'll be limited for space, so choose only the images or words that really speak to you. The Board can be arranged in the way that's most logical for you. My own Board is divided into four areas. In the middle is a picture of my son (feel free to use photos), because he is my main focus in life. Your focus piece doesn't have to be a relative, or even a person. It can be a word or a landscape—anything—just as long it is your primary inspiration, the main reason you want to achieve your dreams. Whatever you choose, it ought to be something that can help you get through hard times just by looking at it. The images on your board can always be changed.

One area of my Board is devoted to my career. My business goals are represented by pictures of huge crowds—crowds I'd like to speak to. I have a personal section with pictures of people I admire, clothes I like, and things I enjoy, like yoga and meditation. I have a section for material things: houses, cars, and planes . . . that's right, planes. I have even taken the liberty of pasting pictures of myself in airplanes, at travel destinations, and on stages.

There is no right way or wrong way to do this, and this is not a place to hold back. It's a Dream Board, not a wish board. The images should serve as reminders of the possibilities. This is not a project that has to be finished all at one time. It should be a continuous work in progress. You're always allowed to change your mind! The following questions will help you to prepare:

Personal _____

_____

_____

_____

_____

Relationships _____

_____

_____

_____

_____

Career/Business _____

_____

_____

_____

_____

Spiritual _____

_____

_____

_____

_____

Material _____

_____

_____

_____

_____

Health _____

_____

_____

_____

_____

Financial _____

_____

_____

_____

_____

When you've answered the questions, begin looking in
the magazines for your images. Don't forget, cut out
any words or phrases that are meaningful to you as
well. Some of the words on my board are:

Just listen
Kindness
Expansion
Fitness
Opportunity
Take charge!
Creativity
Nutrition
Beauty
Stimulating
Brilliant
Dedicated speaker
Trendsetter
Love

These words help me stay focused. If you can't find the words you like in publications, you can always type them up on the computer and print them out, or you can even write them on a piece of paper.

The sooner you begin working on your Dream Board, the sooner you will begin to see the dreams manifesting themselves in your life. When you are finished—or until you begin a new board—place it in a handsome frame. It will lend dignity to your work, like a beautiful piece of art. If you're able, hang it in a place where you will see it daily.

Remember: Successful people do what unsuccessful people aren't willing to do: work long hours, take risks, sacrifice, and hold in mind a dream until it happens. Over and over, people have asked me if I really do all the things that I am asking you to do. "Of course," I say. I have ultimate confidence in them. What I describe to you is exactly what has made me successful. There's no doubt that some people will prefer the Cliff's Notes version of this book. They are cheating themselves, I believe. The truth of the matter is, there are no short cuts to success, as anyone who has achieved it and kept it will tell you. Work is always part of the success equation, and, as they say, the dictionary is the only place where success comes before work.

All of these things take self-leadership. It takes the ability to look deep inside and constantly challenge the very core of who you are. You will master the art of dreaming when you master the art of self-leadership.

Chapter 10

Duplicating Success and Learning from Failure

As you chart your path to your dreams, know that there will be times when the storms of life will seem unbearable. They will beat and grind upon you like a hurricane. Stay the course, and don't lose sight. Remember to do everything possible to keep centered, and always have faith that this, too, shall pass.

• • • • • • • • • • •

One of the toughest lessons I have had to learn in life is being able to accept failure. I spent most of my life running scared, terrified I would fail, and as a result, I usually ended up in the very scenario I was so desperately trying to escape. That, I believe, is the definition of failure. I also believe that this is a vicious cycle almost all of us find ourselves in more often than we'd like. Is it possible to break this cycle? The answer is a resounding YES!

My dear friend and mentor Sande Herron once told me: "You have to make failure your friend. Instead of working against it, you need to work *with* it. You see, it's all in the way you perceive failure. As Zig Ziglar said, 'Failure is an event.'" Throughout life, we are all taught that failure is reflective. It reflects upon us as people— as human beings. This is a false notion. Instead, failure most often reflects the fact that someone is actually attempting to reach a goal, and they are willing to take risks to realize their dreams. Personally, I would rather fail than to go to my grave without having tried everything in my power to succeed.

After my second divorce, I felt like I had failed at every relationship I'd been involved in. I thought there was no way that I could ever love again. But the truth of the matter was, both of my marriages were *events* in my life. It was up to me whether I would learn lessons from these events or not. I've heard it said that human beings continue to repeat mistakes until we finally learn our lessons, and I surely didn't want to go through that kind of pain again. I paid very careful attention to lessons during this period of my life.

We have been taught to respond the most profoundly to the failures in life, or to bad things that happen to us or to other people. We watch news that is full of stories of death and destruction. We read newspapers full of doom and gloom, and we gossip with friends and strangers alike about the horrors of society. It's no wonder that we always look at the cup as being half empty!

Have you ever entertained any of these thoughts?

- I can't.
- I'll fail.
- I will never amount to anything.
- What's the use? Nobody cares.

- It's already been done.
- I am too small, too short, too fat, or too skinny.
- I am not smart enough.
- I can't trust anyone.
- I am too old.
- I am too young.
- I am ugly.
- I am slow.
- It's already been done.
- My business will never make it.
- I am hopeless.

I actually heard a lot of these things, and I certainly told myself many of them. I accepted all of these false statements until I realized I was the one holding the power. Only I could make positive change in my life. Only I could take the initiative to live a life free of fear. In the following exercises, you, too, can learn to combat negative feelings and ideas when they come up.

EXERCISE: IDENTIFYING FAILURES

It's never easy to dwell on our mistakes and failures, but it's also crucially important to recognize and admit to them. On the lines below, write down one to five events that you consider a failure in each of the areas of your life. Take all the time you need, and be honest!

Personal_____

_____

_____

_____

Work/Career _____

_____

_____

_____

_____

Education _____

_____

_____

_____

_____

Relationships _____

_____

_____

_____

_____

Financial _____

_____

_____

_____

_____

This exercise is not intended to cause you to feel badly about yourself. Rather, it is designed to force you to make tough admissions, and then to let them go, so that they won't clutter your mind and your goals any longer.

Take a long, hard look at your entries, and allow yourself to feel. Your feelings may include sadness, anger, fear, rejection, and a lack of self-esteem. This is natural and healthy. As you consider each item you wrote down, try to see it from a "bird's eye" view. If this list belonged to someone else, would you judge them as harshly as you judge yourself? If you had been older and/or wiser, would you have done things differently? Who else was involved in these events? Were the choices you made well thought out, or were they made spontaneously? Were you influenced by outside events or people? Most importantly, can you forgive yourself and move on?

This process can take minutes, hours, or days. In fact, once you become accustomed to analyzing your mistakes, you will spend the rest of your life honing your decision-making skills. For now, though, you must learn to let go. You must actively engage in allowing yourself to be human, and you must stop yourself from using past failures as an excuse not to move forward. The first step in this process seems like a simple one, but it is more powerful than you can imagine.

Let's work on letting go. First, transfer your failure "event" list to a separate sheet of paper. Read it over again, and give each item your full attention. Say each entry out loud, and then, aloud, say, "This was just an event. It's over now. I have learned from my mistake, and now I can purge this from my life."

Now it's time to physically destroy these harmful and self-defeating "events." How you do it is up to you, but it's important to make the process ritualistic. You can tear the sheet of paper into a hundred pieces and throw it in the trash. You can take it out to the barbeque grill and set it on fire. You can flush it down the toilet. You can even lay the paper down in your driveway and run the car over it a dozen times! The more dramatic, the better! The idea is to destroy that which is holding you back.

Learning to regard failure as a lesson for success isn't easy. We have all been preprogrammed from childhood to dwell on the negative. This is something you will have to practice. So many valuable things can be learned when we allow ourselves to remove the negative emotions that are tied to failure. You must promise yourself that you will only regard failure as a means to self-improvement.

• • • • • • • • • • •

When the pain becomes unbearable, the decision is made.
Make sure you are making the decision.

• • • • • • • • • • •

When my son was first learning to walk, I would watch in amazement as he took a step, fell, and then got back up and did it again. Parents understand that watching their children fail hurts them a lot more than it hurts their children. I learned a tremendous amount from my son about determination. Can you imagine if, as young children, we gave up as soon as we realized that falling down hurt? We would all still be crawling! That is a very literal example of how frightening failure can be, but figuratively speaking, the majority of teenagers and adults are still experiencing this same fear, and it is holding them back from stepping into their greatness. If we never stand up and take a chance, we'll never know what wonderful things may lie ahead of us. We are scared to jump off the proverbial cliff, so we stay quietly sitting on a bench, watching life pass us by. When we finally work up the courage, we find the cliff wasn't nearly as steep or scary as we'd ever imagined!

Exercise: Celebrating Our Successes

So how do we make failure work for us? We begin by celebrating our successes, hard as it might be. It can be hard for some people because they find it easier to identify with failure and much more difficult to list their successes on paper. This is where we leave our humble feelings behind and embrace our achievements. In essence, we are doing the opposite kind of exercise we performed above.

Again, take your time, be honest, and write down the things you have done that make you proud.

Personal _____

_____

_____

Work/Career _____

_____

Education _____

_____

Relationships _____

_____

Financial _____

_____

One of the most important things I have mastered is the art of reflective thinking. Reflective thinking means going back in time and connecting to an event that resulted in success. If I can bring that victorious feeling to the forefront of my mind, I can use it again to inspire greatness in the present.

In Chapter 1 and some of the following chapters, I have referred to an event that happened almost twenty-five years ago: running and winning an 880-yard race when I was just a boy. It was one of the most formative events of my life because I learned to tame the preprogrammed negative voice that had haunted me for so long. I still summon that memory often when I am feeling down and need to lift my spirits. I think back to that day, and I connect to the following ideas:

1. What was I feeling in the seconds before the race?
2. What characteristics did I demonstrate (bravery, commitment, fearlessness)?
3. How did I feel afterward?

When I allow myself to accept that I was able to create success then, I realize that I can create success in the situation I am in NOW. That's when I'm able to ACT. That's when I'm able to MOVE. I reflect, I listen to my inner voice, and then I perform. This exercise has gotten me through more difficult times than I can count, and it can work for you, too!

Return to your "success" list now, and allow your mind to open to your potential greatness. Run through the list and try to remember any detail of the event you can. The more details you can remember about your success, the more you can duplicate that success.

Ask yourself the following questions in regard to each of your successes:

1. What was I feeling when this event went so well?
2. How was I behaving (brave, committed, fearless)?
3. How did I feel afterward?

Try to be as detailed as possible.

Personal _____

_____

_____

Work/Career _____

_____

_____

Education _____

_____

_____

Relationships _____

_____

_____

Financial _____

_____

_____

Life happens quickly, and we rarely take the time to sit back and enjoy our individual triumphs. Ironically, there is perhaps nothing more important to ultimate success. Once you have completed this exercise, please take a few minutes and enjoy the remembrance of the accomplishments you've created in your life, whether you are a Fortune 500 executive, a housewife, or a student. We can only benefit by identifying with our successes.

When I was creating Imagine 2002, it seemed that every conceivable hurdle came my way. In the past, I may well have given up. This time, though, I became ever more determined to make the event a reality. Many times I sat in my office, closed my eyes, and heard that gun go off, signaling thirty young boys to take off running. I savored the sound of the cheering crowd as I crossed the finish line, and I applied that feeling to my current situation. Other days I would sit and return to the day I flew my boss to Mexico in a private plane, or maybe I'd fill my senses with the view from the top of the Eiffel Tower. The point was to feel as if I could, and would, conquer the world, come hell or high water. Connecting to that powerful part of me would always give me the strength to carry on. We all have the ability to do the same. We must learn to think of past accomplishment and success and build on them rather than identifying with our failures.

• • • • • • • • • •

Every day for many years, a man prayed to God that he would win the lottery. After many months, God finally answered back: "Come on! Help out a little bit! Go out and buy a ticket!"—Anonymous

• • • • • • • • • •

Throughout most of my life, during the times when I felt like a failure, I was really going through a learning process, although I didn't necessarily know it at the time. It wasn't until later in life that I was able to tie success and failure together to make them a "power duo."

Life might be considered a huge canvas; every time we add the wrong color or the wrong brushstroke, we must take a moment to understand that one simple misstep often takes us in the direction we were seeking the whole time. In other words, everything happens for a reason. The task is to learn the lesson, not to question the event.

EXERCISE: THE RF METHOD

I have been asked many times, "How do you get out of something when you are stuck?" My answer is, "I have a very powerful exercise that helps me get motivated in the right direction." It has now become natural for me to use the tools that I have learned along the way to reap personal and professional rewards. There is one particular process, however, that I have used over and over again. It gets very powerful results for me. I call it the RF Method of reaching success.

I mentioned the art of reflective thinking above. I define it as going back to a place in time when you enjoyed success of some type, reidentifying with it, and reengaging your energy for the future. Too many times we allow failure to paralyze us and destroy our ambitions. The RF Method of success is a simple process, but it requires you to act.

When I was in the midst of creating the first Latino success forum, one overriding thing proved to be true: There were always plenty of people, places, and tasks that would distract me from my actual goal, and I would find myself wondering why I was getting caught up in what was basically meaningless. Many times our failures are not a result of a lack of good intentions; they come about because we have allowed something to distract us from what is really important.

The four basic tenets of the RF Method are:

Reconnect—Focus
Recommit—Focus
Rediscover—Focus
Reengage—Focus

Reaching success is a constant redirection of our goals. Give this experiment a try: Stand outside and pick out a tree in your yard or in a park. Now stand directly in line with that tree. Every time you take a step toward that tree, you must redirect your goal to reach that tree. In our daily lives we have thousands of thoughts running through our minds at one time. If we allow our thoughts to wander, we are likely to find ourselves in the yard next door! The RF Method of success will allow you to stay focused, even during the most turbulent times.

When you find yourself in a place where you feel lost, like you are failing, like you are disconnected from your goals, take a few minutes and reconnect to the reason you are attempting that goal in the first place. Find a place where you won't be bothered, and turn off all the chatter of the world surrounding you. This exercise is meant to be a connection with *you*, not with the outside world. It amazes me when I see people so connected to their cell phones, pagers, and laptops, who then wonder why they aren't connected to themselves. Turn the distractions off, and answer the following questions:

- If you are a student, why are you going to school? Why did you go to all the trouble of applying to an institution of learning? What are your goals?

_____

_____

_____

_____

_____

_____

- If you are a business owner, what led you to become involved in the business you are in? What were your initial goals for starting this business? What are your ultimate goals?

_____

_____

_____

_____

_____

- If you are an employee, why did you choose your particular job? Do you have aspirations beyond this work? Why did you accept this position? Are you satisfied and proud of your work?

_____

_____

_____

_____

_____

_____

Reconnecting. It is extremely important that we understand the "why" behind our dreams. Otherwise we end up wondering whether we are leading our lives or our lives are leading us. Once you have truly identified the "why," you can reconnect to your life goals. We all sway from our original dreams—we change our minds and we rethink what we want from life. It's only natural. Reconnecting with what we want in the here and now serves to remind us what we are capable of and what we deserve from life. Reconnection will also allow you to perform the next step: refocusing.

Refocusing. Now that you have reconnected with your past, your goals, and your dreams, it's time to refocus. We must clearly see what it is we want, and we must make mental and physical efforts to get there. Success requires purpose, and it is only by focusing that we can harness that purpose and make it work for us. We must recognize why we are drawn to a certain journey in life, and we must not be swayed from our mission. We must see the tree, we must focus on the tree, and we must now recommit our individual steps.

Recommitting. Many times we allow the fear of failure to take us out of the game. Then all of a sudden we find ourselves losing that focus we worked so hard on. It happened to me over and over again. I reiterate: Life is so full of distractions that giving into the chatter can literally mean the end of your aim. When this happens, you must force yourself to get back in the game, which can be difficult. It takes a will of steel and a renewed effort to reconnect, refocus, and recommit. Assess the results you have seen so far and celebrate them. Assess your failures, forgive yourself, learn from them, and move on.

EXERCISE: ACTIONS SHOW COMMITMENT

Take a few minutes and write down the actions you have taken that show commitment toward your goals. Remember, commitment means action. What are you willing to do to get where you want to go?

_____

_____

_____

_____

_____

_____

_____

We must reconnect and refocus in order to reach our goals. Taking action is how we prove our commitment. It is a cyclical process: You make a commitment, you refocus again, you reconnect, you commit, you refocus. It can be frustrating, it can feel like a chore, it can be easily ignored. But it can also bring fulfillment and joy like you have never experienced.

The last step in the process is to rediscover your passion; rediscover the greatness in you that created results in the past. Reidentify with the powerful you—the one who began this journey in the first place—the one who had enough passion to form a powerful dream.

In order to nurture your passion, you must rediscover yourself every day. Without passion, it is nearly impossible to remain motivated. Without passion, it is very difficult to recruit the help you need on your journey, too, for passion is contagious.

There are some men who have a hard time admitting that they are passionate beings. Do you consider yourself passionate? Or are you allowing failure to get the best of you? The goal of the following exercise is to rediscover that emotion that resonates deep within your soul.

EXERCISE: YOUR TRUE PASSIONS

Take a few moments to write down your true passions. There are no right or wrong answers: Your passions belong to you alone.

I am passionate about _____

_____

_____

_____

_____

_____

_____

Your passions should tell you very important things about your dreams. Look at your list carefully, and consider whether your current situation reflects what is truly important to you. Now focus on how to get the results that would enhance your life, and reengage your efforts toward those goals.

There is a great scene in the movie *Top Gun*. In fact, Tom Cruise's fly-boy character engages in the RF Method with great results, although I can't take credit! In one scene, Cruise's character is in combat with the enemy. He is flying wing man, and his job is to protect the lead plane. In the heat of battle, he loses his composure and can't follow through with his mission. He bails out, leaving his team vulnerable to destruction. In the film, his character goes through a constant inner struggle that paralyzes him into utter inaction. Then, just when you think he's out for the count, he reconnects, refocuses, recommits, and rediscovers his passion. He steps into his greatness and reengages in the fight, coming out a hero.

Reengaging in our dreams and goals is imperative. All along life's travels, people will say, "You can't." Your friends and family may not understand your dreams;

they may be afraid for you. But the truth of the matter is, it is not their wall to climb. It is yours. So keep on climbing!

Chapter 11

Self-Leadership

*I refuse to give up—not because I'm proud,
but because I believe in my dreams, and I
know that what God has begun in me, He
will finish. That is what changes me.*

. . . .

As I look back at my life and where my journey has
taken me, it is clear that everything I experienced was
for me. In other words, nothing happened *to* me but *for*
me. I know now that self-leadership and responsibility
are by far the greatest lessons we can learn in creating
the results we are looking for in our lives. Our world
today is full of finger-pointing. Maybe it's always been
that way. The general thinking is that anything that goes
wrong is everyone's fault but our own. Self-leadership
takes the responsibility for success out of the hands of
people and things outside of us and places it where it
belongs—in our hands. When we become aware of this,
we can then see that all lessons in life are for our greater
understanding of greater goals.

I recently visited Dallas, Texas, to speak to a group of

parents who had gathered at a local high school to talk about their kids' behavior. The parents seemed to blame the school system for anything their children did that displeased them. In all honesty, I sat there in amazement, listening to these adults justify their children's acts and words, speaking as if the school was a training ground for heathens and evildoers. When it was time for me to speak, I took the podium and told them frankly that if they didn't like the way their kids were acting, they should go home and look in the mirror. In so many words, I insisted that the blame lay not with the school but at home. In the next few minutes, you could have heard a pin drop. It was dead silent.

As adults, it is imperative that we understand that everything in our lives is either a direct or indirect result of our own actions—not someone else's. If those parents had taken the time, which is a considerable commitment, to raise their children correctly, to actually be a part of their lives, I'm certain they would not have needed to be in that meeting that night.

· · · · · · · · · · ·

Self-leadership is all about understanding one very important thing: We were all born with greatness, and it is our duty to not only accept that fact but to proactively "step into" that greatness. When we do so, we are saying to our creator that we are willing to live our lives with purpose. Our world would be a very different place if we quit being victims and started living our lives as if they have meaning, as if everything we do is on purpose.

When I went through my second divorce, I had to take a very hard look at my own part in the relationship and its problems and failures. I had to realize and admit that I was the common denominator in all of the events that had happened in my life. No person or thing remained the same throughout all of the situations I had experienced except for me, myself, and I. It was, as I have mentioned throughout this book, the most formative and life-changing realization I have ever made. It let me know something that scared me and gave me comfort all at the same time. I had to take full responsibility for myself and for the things that happened in my life.

Accepting your greatness is about having the ability to stand in front of a mirror, look into your eyes, and love what you see, no matter what. It is about not desiring to be anyone different than who you are and who you were born to be. In order to achieve goals and dreams, whatever they may be, we must be willing to recognize and accept where we are at any given moment. When you connect to the greatness within you at that moment, you then give yourself the power to make and create change. When I realized and *accepted* that I, Daniel Gutierrez, was the world's premier Latino motivator and that that was what I had been born to be, I finally gave myself permission to step into my greatness. I *accepted* that power, and I was able to move forward, rather than holding myself back with self-doubt and placing blame elsewhere.

Stepping into greatness is about living your dreams and passion, no matter what they may be. It's about not waiting for the world to tell you that you're great; it's about telling the world that you're great and continuing to believe it until the whole world "gets" it.

I'm often asked who made me the World's Number One Latino Motivator. I answer that I did! People who have known me for some time would laugh if they heard me make such a large claim, but I honesty *believe* that I am the World's Number One Latino Motivator. I was invited to attend a breakfast for professionals a few years ago. As the meal was wrapping up, my host introduced me by saying, "I want to thank Mr. Daniel Gutierrez for his support of our organization. Mr. Gutierrez is the World's Number One Latino Motivator!" I smiled and thought to myself, "Okay! Now people are catching on. Now the world is beginning to see my vision!"

EXERCISE: LOOKING IN THE MIRROR

If you haven't caught on yet, this is an interactive book. Usually that term is applied to computers, but think about the parts of that word: *inter* and *active.* Action is so important. Every monument begins with a single stone; every successful life begins with a dream. The key is moving forward (action) and working with other people. It's about finding the sources you need, whether it be information, contacts, faith, or your dreams.

Right now I'm going to ask you to take several actions that will help you to recognize your greatness so that you can move forward. First of all, put this book down and find a mirror. If you can't find a hand mirror, take this book and use a wall mirror.

Some people may find it easy to look in the mirror, but many more do not. It naturally makes us feel uncomfortable. Why? Because we are afraid to really see ourselves—to confront that face, eye to eye, and think about what we see. Try to slow your thoughts by breathing slowly and deeply, and keep reminding yourself that you are doing this for a very good reason. When you are feeling calm and your breathing is regulated, look directly into your own eyes.

Inside of every one of us is the little boy or girl we once were. Guess what? One of the few things you still share with that child is your eyes. While you are looking in the mirror, try to imagine yourself at the age of five or so. Think about what you looked like then, how you dressed, how your hair was cut and most importantly, how you felt. Your ultimate goal in this exercise is to connect to that little girl or little boy. He or she has been lost for a very long time. You won't be able to accept your greatness until you are able to connect to that child inside.

• • • • • • • • • • •

Connection to others is very important, but connection to self is crucial to growth and understanding of the world around us. For it is when we are connected to ourselves that we understand the meaning of our existence.

• • • • • • • • • • •

This connection may be elusive at first. It may take a while before you are able to feel that child and listen to what that child has to say. It takes a lot of practice and concentration. Your ability to master this exercise will launch you forward into a new level of success you've only dreamed of before.

A few years ago, I coached a young lady who was over-weight. She was by all standards very successful. She was twenty-five, she was a real estate broker, she owned property, she owned her own business (which grossed $25,000 a month). It appeared on the outside as if ev-erything in her life was just fine. But it wasn't. In fact, the opposite was true. This lovely and intelligent woman was absolutely miserable. And there was one thing she couldn't do. She couldn't look at herself in the mirror. She was so embarrassed by her weight that she had actually gone so far as to remove all of the mirrors in her home so she would never have to look at herself. After coaching her for some time, I finally told her that if she didn't accept herself the way she was—overweight— she would never be happy.

Earlier I had asked her to make a list of all the things she wanted to accomplish. To her dismay, when she gave me the list, I ripped it in half. I told her that none of the items on the list would be possible until she faced her toughest mountain: herself. She had to face that the 300 pounds she was carrying around was, in fact, *her.* In order to change anything in her life, she would first have to look in the mirror and face herself as she was.

To my delight, she did just that. With my encourage-ment and prodding, she finally gained the courage to acknowledge her physical state. Soon after, within days in fact, the magic of self-acceptance took over. Cynthia got honest with herself, lost her fear and denial, and took action. Today she weighs 170 pounds. Her goal is 140, and she will certainly attain it. She now has the most important tool: self-acceptance. All she had to do was look in the mirror and face herself; her world changed completely as a result of that simple action. We all have this power. Now it's your turn!

After you have tried this simple yet often intimidating step of looking in the mirror, searching your eyes (the window to your soul) for the perfect and innocent child you hold within, and taking the first steps toward loving and accepting the truth and yourself, take some time to write down how you felt about the experience.

Though you should practice the mirror exercise as often as you can, you don't need to write about it every time. A bit later, we'll be talking about journaling. This is a first step.

Looking in the mirror made me feel like _____

_____

_____

_____

_____

_____

_____

_____

_____

The Seven Golden Rules

Along life's path, with all of its ups and downs, I have stuck to seven golden rules to help me keep moving forward. In previous chapters I described in detail what my days were like while trying to plan a major event. You saw the ups and downs very clearly! By including my journals of that time, I wanted to give you a real look at what chasing a dream looks like. I will never tell you that chasing your dreams is easy, but I will say that we all have the capacity to do so! The golden rules that follow will help you on your way.

• • • • • • • • • •

Following your dreams is never easy. But think about the regrets you'd have if you reached the end of your life without having tried.

• • • • • • • • • •

Rule 1: Let Go of Your Limited Beliefs

As a young boy, I started out life believing that I was a failure because I had let my mother down. The truth of the matter was, I was just a little boy! What could I have done? In those days, there were no 911 operators to call. In order to become successful, I had to let go of the belief that I was a failure, and I had to replace it with a positive affirmation: I loved my mother and I had done the best I could. What is your limited belief about yourself? Write it down on a sheet of paper, and then counter that belief with something positive. You may have ten of them, and you might just have one. Use the following model.

Limited belief _____

Positive affirmation _____

Once you do this, hang the sheet of paper where you can see it every day. In combination with the mirror exercise, continue to remind yourself about all of your positive attributes until you really believe them!

Rule 2: Let Go of the Past

This step may take some time and patience, but it is a necessary step if you want to move forward and create the type of life you are dreaming of.

On a very hot summer day I attended a seminar that forced me to deal with the feelings I had for my father. Boy, did I feel the heat. I hadn't seen him in decades, and I had only one memory of him: the dreadful night when he tried to kill my mother. I had never been to his grave, and before that day I didn't even care. This seminar changed everything, though. I was now compelled to meet my father. I called my sister the next day, and she mailed me the location of the place where my dad had been buried in Homestead, Florida.

With some encouragement from some very good friends, I bought a ticket to Homestead. I had never been there, and I had no idea what to expect. I was admittedly very scared and very nervous about making the trip. It was a long trip to my past so that I could confront the father I never knew and I could ask the question, Why?

The day I was due to leave, I had my friends take me to the airport just to make sure I actually got on the flight. I was afraid I would chicken out if I didn't have someone to hold me accountable. When the moment came, and I was on my way to Florida to face my past, I knew there was no going forward until I was able to deal with the haunting questions I needed to ask. When I arrived, the air was oppressively humid. I was tired because I had taken a red-eye and traveled all night. But the fear and excitement kept my adrenalin pumping. I looked at a map and saw that the cemetery was a 45-minute drive south. For a split second, I thought about returning the car and getting on the plane back to L.A. Instead I moved forward. What happened that day would change my life forever.

I pulled into the cemetery parking lot. There was one problem. How would I find my father in this huge place? I sat in the car with tears welling up in my eyes wondering what to do. Suddenly there was a man at my window. In an authoritative voice he asked, "May I help you, son?" I almost rubbed my eyes like a disbelieving cartoon character. There, standing in front of me, was the priest who worked at the grounds chapel. I identified him as a priest because he wore a white clerical collar and a black suit. It just so happened that he was there meeting with a family. The fact that he was a priest gave me great comfort. I looked at him like the five-year-old boy I'd once been who'd lost his father. "I'm looking for my daddy. Can you help me?" I managed. He smiled warmly. "Of course, son," he replied. Then he led me to the office so the clerk could look up the name.

After some time she located his plot and asked me if I wanted help finding his grave, and then walked me there. It seemed like hours had passed as we crossed the grass; in reality, it was only minutes. I decided to wait before I approached the gravesite. The kind woman told me where I could find her if I needed anything and left me for some private time.

It took me a while to gather my courage. Thirty minutes later, I took the first step. Soon I was reading his name: John Victor Gutierrez. I just stared, and then I began to cry—the tears of a lost little boy. Standing there, I was five years old again, and I let my emotions and questions pour forth: "Where were you when I needed you most?" I whispered. Then my voice got louder. "Why the hell were you so mean to my mother?" I sat down, suddenly exhausted. Then it happened, the moment that changed everything. All of a sudden, I realized that I had become the man that I'd always wanted to be. There I was, a grown man. I dried my tears and I just talked to my dad as if he was right there listening. I told him how proud he would be.

Time had stopped for me, and then I realized that I had come on this long journey not to find my dad but to find myself. The tears flowed again as all those years of hate turned to love. My pain dissipated and I forgave him, and in that forgiveness I forgave myself as well.

I pulled the vase off of his gravestone, and I dusted it

off. I wanted to leave him better than I had found him. I had passed a Wal-Mart on the way, so I got in my car, went to the store, and bought him some silk flowers so that he would always have them. As I was leaving the store, I looked over to my right and saw a brightly colored bird on a stick with wings that rotated in the wind. I smiled inside and bought the bird, too.

I drove back to the cemetery filled with excitement over my profound discovery of forgiveness, but that wasn't the last surprise of the day. I returned to his grave and placed the flowers in the vase. The day had been very still, with no wind at all, but when I put the bird in the vase, as soon as I let go, the wind picked up and the wings on the bird began to "fly." In the quiet cemetery, the only sound I heard was that of the bird's wings. I smiled and said, "I hear you, Daddy." It was as if he was saying, "I'm proud of you, son," something I had longed to hear for so many, many years.

For the first time in my life, I was glad that he had been born. For if he hadn't, neither would I! Everyone has a purpose on this earth, and I believe his was to have three children: me, my brother, and my sister. I realized in that moment that his life echoed through me. It was now my purpose on this earth to change lives. He would always live through me.

I flew back the next morning. As I was reading the paper, I realized that the day before had been Father's Day. It had escaped my mind completely. I silently cried again as the plane taxied down the runway, taking me back to Los Angeles a changed man. "Happy Father's Day, Dad," I prayed.

Letting go of the past breaks the chains that bind us. It frees us so that we can find the true purpose of our lives. What are you harboring in your past? Isn't it time you let it go? In the space below, write down the things from your past that keep you from stepping into your greatness.

_____

_____

_____

_____

_____

_____

Rule 3: Take Charge of Your Thinking

If you say to yourself, "I can't," then you're right. If you say to yourself, "I can," you're also right! The power of thought is so immense it can direct the course of your life.

Many times we find ourselves in places that are undesirable, and we wonder how we got there. I would say that our thoughts have a lot to do with it. Our internal dialogue plays an essential role in our pursuit of success, determining not only our ability to reach success but to keep it. What you say to yourself dictates your future.

I was asked by a friend to read the book *Think and Grow Rich* by Napoleon Hill. When I saw the book title I automatically said to myself, "What a scam! No one can think and grow rich!" As a result of that thinking, I decided not to take my friend's advice. Later, down the road, when I was going through some tough times. I was desperate to try anything that would get me out of the funk I was in. I remembered the book my friend had mentioned, and I went and bought it. It was the best $5.95 I ever spent, and I still read it on a monthly basis.

What I learned was: We do have the power of thought. It is the one thing that separates us from animals and the one thing that separates us from our fellow man.

Here's an example: In 2002, I was invited to attend a business gala in Los Angeles. I was very excited to be included in such a prestigious event, which was held at the Century City Westin Plaza Hotel. I asked my girlfriend to attend with me, and she put on her best dress, while I donned a fancy black tuxedo. Off I went, with the idea that I would meet people who would surely further my career. That excitement was quashed when we arrived and were assigned table 56. I looked everywhere for table 56. When I finally found it, it was tucked so far back in the room it might as well have been in the kitchen. My seat actually abutted the back wall.

As we sat down, my date said, "I guess you aren't as important as you thought." I could have let the comment ruin my night, but I didn't. Instead I looked at the other couple at the table and I said, "Do you know that you are sitting at the most important table in the room?" They looked at me as if I'd lost my mind. I wasn't done, though. "Mark my words. The next time I am in this room, I will be the master of ceremonies!" They just smiled warily, probably hoping I'd shut up. That night

George Lopez and Selma Hayek entertained us, and we enjoyed a nice dinner.

Two years later, I received a letter from that same business organization asking me to be a master of ceremonies for their next event! As I read the letter, I leaned back and remembered the comment I'd made to those incredulous strangers.

On the night of the event, the lights were dimmed and the energy was high. As our host announced that Daniel Gutierrez would be the master of ceremonies, I stepped on stage and looked at the table at the back of the room where I'd been seated before and smiled to myself. I'd done it; I'd made my dreams come true.

EXERCISE: YOUR INTERNAL DIALOGUE

In the spaces below, write down the internal dialogue you have regarding the five areas of your life indicated. Next, write down a new, more positive internal dialogue. This exercise will make you more aware of your thoughts and will allow you to make changes toward creating the success you seek.

Personal _____

_____

Work/Career _____

_____

Education _____

_____

Relationships _____

_____

Financial _____

_____

You need to pay diligent attention to your internal dialogue. When a thought comes into your mind that is not in alignment with what you really want, you must stop immediately and veto that thought. Change it before it takes over! This takes practice, so don't give up!

Rule 4: Let Go of Your Need to Be Right

We can all have what we want if we can let go of what we think something is "supposed" to look like.

· · · · · · · · · · ·

When I was producing Imagine 2002, one of the things I had to do was to let go of being right about what the event was supposed to look like. I needed to learn to be more flexible—to change what I had in my mind in order to get what I wanted.

Sometimes we hang on to our beliefs so tightly that our need to be right becomes more important than the actual results we are looking for. Our businesses, our dreams, and our relationships with others need room to modify and grow. Allow them that freedom!

Take a look at the different areas in your life. Are you getting the results you are looking for? If not, is the problem that your need to be right is overriding everything else?

Below, write down the things you perceive as "right." Then, after some thought, write down ways you can compromise and expand your horizons.

EXERCISE: LETTING GO

Personal _____

_____

Work/Career _____

_____

Education _____

_____

Relationships _____

_____

Financial _____

_____

Rule 5: Be the Cause of Your Life

We live in a world where we want everything brought to us. It's as if we sit back in our chairs and expect life to "do us" instead of "us doing life."

In order for you to reach the level of success that you desire, you must get off the couch and be the cause of your life. In other words, it's up to YOU to make things happen. So many people like to say, "When this happens, I will do so-and-so, and when that happens, I'll do x, y, and z." Then they wonder why the world is not coming to them.

This world operates on universal laws, one being that action creates an equal or opposite reaction. If you sit on your couch waiting all day for the phone to ring, what will you get? Your house repossessed! If there is no action in your life, you must create it yourself. When I decided that I was going to run that 880-yard race in high school, I didn't wait for the coach to ask. I took it upon myself to get the right shoes and jump right in. When I decided that I wanted to finance the Mexican nationals in my Best Buy store, I didn't wait for someone to ask me. Instead, I began researching and I began moving toward my goal.

If you have an idea you want to bring to market, do it! If you want to attend a particular school but have not been asked, apply! If you want to date more, then start asking more people! Take some risks! Self-leadership requires that we be willing to create and attract the things that are not coming to us. What are you waiting for?

Rule 6: Be Committed to Your Dreams

We always get what we are committed to. Can you remember the last time you really wanted something and got it? It was because you really were committed to that goal. When we are committed to our goals, we will stop at nothing. If we are not committed, any hurdle that comes our way will deter us. In other words, life isn't a hobby—it's a commitment.

EXERCISE: GOALS AND COMMITMENT

Make a list of all the goals you have reached because you were committed to your dreams. I was committed to having the Imagine 2002 event happen no matter what the sacrifice was. All of us have goals we have reached that took commitment. Look at the list and rate yourself from 1 to 10 on the level of commitment you had to get to your goal. You will find in that list the answer to reaching your goals and stepping into your greatness.

_____   _____
_____   _____
_____   _____
_____   _____
_____   _____
_____

Rule 7: Associate with Positive People

This one never ceases to amaze me. People will complain about the company they keep, and then they keep going back to the same crowd. We must consistently surround ourselves with people who support our dreams and goals, and we must let go of those who cannot.

I have a system I call purging. Once a month, I go through my business cards and relationships and I toss out any that aren't working for me or for them. In other words, you must take a look at your relationships and identify people who, for the most part, waste your time and energy. Purge those individuals or companies! Stop trying to pursue them. That doesn't mean you shouldn't speak to those contacts again; it simply means that you should stop wasting valuable effort. Then look for new relationships to replace the ones you have ended.

I had a friend come to me once when I was upset. I had complained to him about new friends and business partners I was pursuing. He looked at me and said, "Daniel, I have known you for a long time, and I have been through thick and thin with you. Am I not a good friend?" I replied, "Of course, you're a great friend. But there is a difference in the way you support me. You support me where I'm at, and they support me in where I want to go. I need people to support me in my greatness."

Sometimes, it is even our friends and family that we need to be able to let go of in order to get to where we need to go. To this day, my family doesn't understand everything I do. That's okay! I love them anyway, and I keep on reaching for my goals so that the entire world can benefit from my desire to inspire and motivate.

Self-leadership is about taking personal responsibility and making necessary changes in your life. It's about thinking outside the box, examining your interior, purging what holds you back, and never saying never.

I was sitting next to a man that had just heard me speak at a conference, and he said, "You know, Daniel, I was thinking about these people in our lives that really just really bring us down and thought of my barber. I hate going to him. He is complaining all day long about life. Yet I find myself going to him every six weeks! I realized today when you talked about purging that I could find another barber to go to."

We all have people like this in our lives. I encourage you to make a list of all the people in your life that you interact with in your personal life and in business. Take a hard look at these people and decide whether they need to be purged and a new relationship be put in their place. Remember that successful people do what unsuccessful people are not willing to do.

Chapter 12

Never, Never, Never Give Up

Living a life of commitment and passion requires walking, and sometimes crawling, but never, never, never giving up.

• • • • • • • • • • •

The most important lesson I learned was from my mother. She demonstrated to me that I should never give up, no matter how bad things got. The funny thing is, she never told me this; she displayed it by her actions. Every day she would come home after working long, hard hours in the field, or working her second job, tired and out of energy. But she still did all the housework and made sure that my brother and sister and I were taken care of. In spite of all the adversity she went through, she never quit doing what she needed to do, which was to provide for her family. We must all have this kind of resolve when it comes to chasing our dreams and passions. Success is up to you. It's all about how much you are willing to tolerate to reach your goal.

I admit that I have not always been proud of where my feet have taken me, but I have never given up hope that God has a greater intention for my life.

My Feet

I am not always proud of where my feet
   have taken me.
I have walked in places most people
   could not understand.
I have been through my own hell and back.
Maybe you have too.
My feet have carried me through places
   of great joy as well.

Please do not look at me strangely
   or judge me because my feet have carried me to places
you have not been or understand.

I mean no harm to you and your loved ones.

I only ask that you love me today,
   not for where my feet have taken me
   but for where they are going.

As I look back at my life, I can see that I've been through a lot. I was a troubled teen who could, in a second, have ended up in prison, especially after I came so close to killing my stepfather. In my twenties, I not only left the security of my faith, I also turned to drugs. I married twice, and both ended in disaster. I've been forced into bankruptcy, and I've lost just about everything. I've been convicted of drunk driving, and I lost my driving privileges for a year. Time and time again, business transactions have failed, leaving me more and more debt.

There were points when I could have thrown in the towel, but there was always something in me that kept saying, "You *are* a winner, and you *can* do it." There were times when I felt lower than an ant's belly, and still, I would find a way to pick myself up, brush myself off, and keep on walking.

If you find yourself in a negative situation, you must understand that there are many people who have felt just like you do. It is human nature for us to feel like we are the only ones going through hardship. When I feel like I am defeated, I read stories of people who have been less fortunate than I. It shows me how relative suffering is. As Dr. Robert Schuller so succinctly expresses it, "Tough times never last, but tough people do!"

Inner Power

Many times I have found myself alone, with just my thoughts, wondering how I will manage to find a way out of my current situation. Time and time again, I have found a creative solution to my troubles. The following are some methods I have discovered for reaching into my inner power and finding answers.

· · · · · · · · · · ·

God speaks to me every day. It's not a question of whether He does or does not, rather it's whether I can hear Him over the chatter of my own thoughts.

· · · · · · · · · · ·

Meditation

One of the most important things we can do is to be in silence. For it is in silence that we are able to listen to that small voice of wisdom and reason.

I had a great coach not too long ago. When I called her up for our first session, I was very stressed about not finding answers to my problems. I began by unloading everything to her. When I finished, she said to me, "Now go out to the pool and sit for four days." I thought my coach had lost her mind! What do you mean sit for four days?

She called me the next day and asked if I had taken her advice. I told her I had not. She was quiet for a moment, and then she said, "Then go out and just sit in silence." Again I thought she was out of her mind! After all, I needed new business to service. How could I go out and just sit? A day later she called again and asked me the same question. Again I said "no." That's when she told me that I would have to find another coach. She said she was only willing to coach me if I was willing to do what she said. She ended the conversation by asking me to call her when my desire to succeed overcame my fear of failing.

The next day, I sat in silence at the pool for what seemed like years. For hours, I just sat there with my thoughts rushing through my mind. The greatest thoughts began to occur on the third day of sitting in silence. The clutter in my mind had finally begun to subside, and I was able to think clearly for the first time in ages. All of a sudden, I was coming up with one solution after another! After the fourth day of sitting, I was absolutely clear on why my coach had asked me to do it. As soon as I was able to stop focusing on the problem and begin focusing on solutions, I found them.

There are many forms of meditation to choose from. I recommend that in the beginning you use a guided meditation on audiotape or CD. It will help you to slow down and be in the silence. Don't be discouraged if at first you can't slow down your thoughts. It takes practice, but the rewards are stupendous.

One of the guided meditations I recommend was created by Dr. Wayne Dyer. The CD comes with a book called *Getting in the Gap*. I use it when I feel like I need help in getting into silence. It's been of immeasurable help to me.

Journaling

I started journaling when I was in high school. At first my expression took form as poetry. Later, it became more of a daily prose account of my life, a diary. Journaling is a great way to get the previous day's problems on paper so that you don't have to carry them into the current day.

I encourage you to go out and buy a journal for yourself. They are available in bookstores and stationery stores. Pick one that you can identify with—there are a variety of formats and binding styles, and you should look through a few before making a decision. Some of my journals have had beautiful covers that inspire me whenever I pick them up. Find one that speaks to you, one that you'll be proud to carry. Before long, your journal will become part of you.

Guidelines for Journaling

- Pick a time in the morning or evening that works for you. Plan to write for at least 30 minutes. In the beginning, you may not be able to write for 30 minutes, but practice makes perfect, and you will be using the time to think as well.
- Write at least three pages every time you journal. If you are like everyone else, writing three pages can be very hard work. When I was blocked, or couldn't seem to find the words to put on paper, I would write "This is stupid" on all three pages! You will find that in the process of journaling, you are removing the layers of blockage that keep you from getting in touch with yourself.
- Learn to write from your heart and not your head. In other words, logic has no place in a journal. This is for you—there is no right way or wrong way to journal. Just get it done.
- Make sure to always date the page, write the time on the page, and where you are at the time. You will find that after a year or so, you can discover what works for you by comparing this information from one journal entry to another. In other words, you can identify places where you are inspired to write, times of day that are most suitable to you, and even certain days of the week that engender your most honest feelings, thoughts, and ideas.

- Make sure that your environment is set up so that you can honestly get real with yourself. I have a vanilla candle and certain music that help me to really reach into the depths of my soul.
- In your journal, dedicate a few pages to your dreams. You can even create a small Dream Board in your journal like the one described in Chapter 9. Go through the same process of cutting out pictures and pasting them into your journal. This will allow you to identify with the dreams you have, and you will be able to connect to what is real for you.
- Break down your journal into quarters: 1st quarter—January to March, 2nd quarter—April to June, 3rd quarter—July to September, 4th quarter—October to December. What this will allow you to do is to focus on one quarter at a time and review your progress in meeting goals you set for that quarter. I believe that we sometimes take on more than we can chew when we look at a task over an entire year. Focus on getting results in the quarter you are in, and take baby steps to create the results you want. This is how corporate America plans and measures business success, and if it is good for corporate America, it is good for individuals too.
- Every day, remember to write down the "yes's" that life presents to you. I have a good friend, Dr. Mark Siegal, who picks up coins every time he sees them on the ground. When he gets home, he tapes the coins to a sheet of paper and writes a story for each coin—a history of sorts. He says, "These coins are

all signs!" I think it's a marvelous idea. Now, every time I see a coin, I pick it up and smile as I think about Dr. Siegal's quest. What the doctor has done is to create a journal of all the coins that remind him of the "yes's" in life. They are all signs that reflect the positives in the world. When you write down even the smallest of things, you end up with a history of all of the good things that happen. At the end of the year you can look back and remind yourself of all these wonderful events. Usually we tend to get to the end of the month and only dwell on what has gone wrong or the bills that are due; we forget all the great things that have happened. Journaling can turn your mind-set around completely. Instead of looking at the year to come as more drudgery, you can be excited about future possibilities!

- Remember that this is your journal. It a a place that you can write your thoughts, goals, concerns, fears, emotions, and commitments. There is no right way or wrong way to journal. Sometimes I use it to think out my business goals; sometimes I just want to get something that has bothered me that day out of my system.

- The magic in journaling is that instead of taking out your aggressions on the world, you have the opportunity to first take them out on paper. I believe you will be amazed by the notion that we can go into tomorrow with a clean slate, that we can learn to see the direction we want to take more clearly.

Understanding and Forgiveness

One of the biggest lessons I have learned along my journey in life concerns understanding and sympathetic awareness. It reminds me of a story:

> A student was seeking out a wise man to answer the questions he had about life. The student looked high and low, looking for the wisest man on earth. He was finally told of a wise man in India, so he decided to sell all of his belongings and make a journey. After many months of looking for this wise man, he finally came upon a fragile old man, the teacher. He was very excited. Now he would have the opportunity to ask his long-held questions. As he entered the room, the wise man asked him why he had made this journey. The student began to tell him the story, and then the wise man stopped him and asked him if he wanted a cup of tea. The student told the wise man, "Sure, but I didn't come here to drink tea!"
> The wise man kept pouring the tea into the cup as the student continued talking. Finally, as he looked down to take a drink, he saw that the teacup was overflowing, and the wise man was still pouring! The student yelled, "Stop! You are spilling tea all over the place!" The wise man stopped and answered, "Yes, you see, the cup is like you, my son. You cannot take in any more truth if you are unwilling to empty your mind and beliefs in order to learn more."

In order to reach the level of success that we are looking for, we must be willing to first empty our "cup" of all the things that have stopped us from being successful. Understanding is about allowing the process of forgiveness to open us up to new ideas and thoughts.

One of the hardest lessons that I have learned is to understand that my family, coworkers, and friends are not always going to be the best people to support me in my dreams. Sometimes it will be because they don't really believe you; it could be that they are jealous; they could be protecting you from harm, and sometimes they just don't understand the burning desire you have to reach your dreams. We must learn to let go of all that and quit looking for validation from other people. Honestly? It may never come. I am sure that many of you, like I did, will continue to go back to our families for validation, only to get what we already have: disappointment.

When I finally accepted that my family is the way they are and that they may not understand my world, I learned to love them exactly the way they are. I forgive them for not understanding my world, and my entire universe opens up for me.

It's not about being right or wrong—it is just what it is—and as soon as we are willing to empty our cup, we learn that we can move on, creating the life we dream of.

Always keep in mind that we are human beings and that forgiveness and understanding are essential to our developing the ability to empty the cup and make room for the good things in life. Holding on to people, places, and things because of what you surmise they may have for you is just keeping you from reaching your full potential.

EXERCISE: TAKING INVENTORY

This is a good place to stop and reflect on things or people in your life that you have not understood and

that you have not forgiven. This is the sort of thing
you can write in your journal. Take an inventory of
those people, places, and things that are keeping you
from reaching success. Write them down and use this
as an opportunity to address your feelings. Then do
the most important thing you can do: Forgive yourself
for anything—I mean anything—that keeps you bound
in chains. Write your inventory in the spaces below.

_____

_____

_____

_____

_____

_____

_____

_____

_____

_____

_____

    Now that you have finished the exercise, go back
and take action. Find a journal and mark the quarter
you are in. Write down what you are going to do to be
more understanding and more forgiving. You will, in
this process, begin to find out who you really are, and
you can begin to identify with yourself and accepting
your greatness.

Being Grateful

I have found that life is unable to give more until we are willing to be grateful for what we have. I have to constantly remind myself to be grateful for everything I have. As I stated earlier, life doesn't happen *to* us, but *for* us.

Everything should be looked at as a blessing.

We must find the good in everything!

I have days when I think nothing else could possibly go wrong. On those days, I stop and make a list of things I am grateful for, and I encourage you to do the same. Don't forget that it is you who are breathing, you who should be grateful. If you are clothed, you should be grateful. If your teeth are brushed, you should be grateful. If you have food on the table you should be grateful. I think this poem says it best (author unknown).

> To realize the value of ONE YEAR, ask a student who has failed a grade.
>
> To realize the value of ONE MONTH, ask a mother who gave birth to a premature baby.
>
> To realize the value of ONE WEEK, ask the editor of a weekly newspaper.
>
> To realize the value of ONE HOUR, ask the lovers who are waiting to meet.
>
> To realize the value of ONE MINUTE, ask a person who has missed a train.
>
> To realize the value of ONE SECOND, ask a person who just avoided a car accident.
>
> To realize the value of ONE MILLISECOND, ask the person who won a silver medal in the Olympics.

Take time now to write down all that you are grateful for in the space below:

_____

_____

_____

_____

_____

_____

_____

_____

_____

_____

_____

Persistence (Never, Never, Never Give Up!)

Lack of persistence can be one of the major reasons that people don't reach the level of success they want. Throughout my life, in times when I thought I was defeated, it was my persistence that allowed me to look deep inside myself and keep on keeping on, even if it meant crawling.

Most people are not willing to go to that level of commitment to achieve their dreams. They would rather be "right" about what they believe.

No matter who you are, what your skill set is, what color you are, or where you come from, you have what it takes on the inside to create the successes in life you are looking for. You must learn to climb over your failures.

• • • • • • • • • • •

Life is tough? Then do life tough!—Les Brown

• • • • • • • • • • •

Four Tips to Staying Persistent in Following Your Dreams

1. *Know where you are going.* One of the toughest decisions I ever made concerned what I really wanted to do in life. There are so many distractions in life that can detour you from your commitment. Even if you aren't sure where you want to go, it's best if you start walking—in the process of walking, you will find your path.

2. *Believe in yourself.* If the whole world tells you that you're crazy, and you do not believe in yourself, you will eventually believe them. You have to be so persistent in what you believe that the whole world shifts. I call myself the World's Number One Latino Motivator. I can remember the first time I said it out loud. It was kind of strange, but in time I really believed it! I told my mother that I was a Latino motivator, and she said, "What? A Latino what? I never heard of such a thing. Daniel, do you have a job?" I smiled and said, "Yes, mother, I'm a Latino motivator!" She replied, "Do they pay you?" I said, "Yes, mother!"

Of course, at the time that wasn't true. I was speaking for free, and on one occasion after speaking, I went out to my car to leave and realized that I didn't have the money to exit the parking lot! I'm sure glad I was able to convince the attendant to let me out or maybe I'd still be there! Today there are books published with my name on the cover, and my tag line is the World's Number One Latino Motivator!

3. *Form a team around you.* You have to be held accountable for your dreams. In order to stay persistent in your endeavors, find a group of people you can meet with from time to time to share your ideas. Tell them it's okay for you to be held accountable. It's best not to use family members for this purpose. Families have a way of telling us what we want to hear rather than what we need to hear. That's why we go to them. Make sure that your team is committed to assisting you to the point of making you angry if they need to. I have several people in my life that will, in a second, let me know when I am off track or in need of redirection.

4. *Create the habit of being persistent.* Practice makes perfect. Just make sure that whatever you are practicing is what you want to be perfect at. We must have courage to make our dreams a reality. We must have resolve that we can achieve a great calling. I know that every experience I have had to endure and the pain of getting through it have taught me the habit of persistence.

Do Your Homework

There is no such thing as a free ride. You must be willing to put in the time that it will take to reach the level of success you are looking for. You must be willing to start at the bottom and work your way up, if that's what it takes. You must be willing to go to school and study, sometimes for years, just to get the opportunity to work at a desired company or profession. You must be willing to do as Jorge Pinos, Sr., Vice President of William Morris in Los Angeles, said to me at a recent luncheon. The following is from my journal of that day.

Two Minutes of Greatness

I had the pleasure of having lunch with Jorge Pinos today. During our conversation, he shared his life experiences with me. What impressed me most was his commitment to excellence. As a young man, he played basketball. He was not a starter, but he practiced for more than four hours every day. I asked, "Why would you work out four hours a day to sit on the bench?"

"I practiced for the two minutes I got to play," he said. "In those two minutes, I showed them my greatness."

We must all remember that in life we will not always get the opportunity to "start" in our desired areas. However, you must practice your skill so that when you get your two minutes, you are ready to step into your greatness.

We are all born with greatness in us. It is up to us to decide to step into that greatness and create the lives that our creator has planned for us. In the end, no matter who you are and what you are facing, success is up to you.

Chapter 13

Protect Your Greatest Asset
—Your Health

*Are our cars more important than our
bodies? Not if we can't drive them.*

. . . .

Our Health and Success

Stepping into greatness is not only about emotional, mental, and financial health—it's about physical health as well. In order to carry out our dreams and goals, we must have the energy to do so!

You must apply the same methods of reaching success to your health. Just like chasing your dreams and passions, it is a constant redirection of your goals and intentions as they pertain to a healthier body. I decided when my son was born that I wanted to be around as long as I could. I have been making changes to my diet ever since. I will be the first to tell you that changing your eating habits is not easy, but what is the alternative? Poor health, lack of energy, or even death?

I make an attempt daily to eat five servings of fruits and vegetables. Like the normal American, I know that it can be challenge. Stepping into greatness requires a great deal of self-leadership: the kind of self-leadership that allows us to examine our very thoughts and intentions and how we execute them. We must be willing to look into the mirror—into our own eyes—and ask ourselves if we are willing to do what it requires to be successful. In the end, success is up to you.

In a survey taken by the *Wall Street Journal,* nine men and one woman, all with very distinguished careers and all very successful by their own right, were asked a series of questions. The questions were intended to discover whether successful people would have done anything differently in their lives if they had the opportunity to go back and change things. Amazingly, nine out of ten answered the same way: They all had agreed that if given the chance to live their lives over again, they would be more attentive to their health.

Many of us spend our entire lives chasing our dreams, and we focus too little time on our physical and mental health, only to struggle during the latter part of our lives to buy it back. To some of you, this may seem outside the realm of your consciousness, especially if you are still in high school or college. However, it was during those very years that I challenged fate by ingesting drugs and drinking too much. I inflicted the wear and tear on my body that I still experience today—to an even greater degree. Tomorrow comes very fast; the things we do to our bodies when we are young quickly and certainly affect our health in the future.

Recent headlines in a number of newspapers and magazines have sounded the alarm. Obesity, diabetes, cancer, heart disease, and high blood pressure are adversely affecting people across the board in numbers we've never seen before! The most worrisome of these killer diseases is diabetes. I read an article recently in *Southwest Spirit,* the in-flight magazine of Southwest Airlines, titled "Diabetes: Diffusing an Epidemic." The major facts pointed out included the following:

- Diabetes is America's sixth leading cause of death, with approximately 210,000 deaths per year.
- Diabetes shortens life expectancy by up to 20 years.
- Diabetes is the leading cause of heart disease, blindness, and limb amputation.
- An American infant born in 2000 has a one-in-three chance of developing diabetes.
- About 29 million Americans will be diagnosed with the disease by 2050.
- An estimated 16 million people have a condition known as "pre-diabetes." About 10 percent of them will develop full-blown diabetes each year.
- African Americans and Latinos have almost twice the risk for Type 2 (non-insulin-dependent) diabetes as the majority of Americans do.
- Diabetes costs the country about 132 billion dollars annually, counting direct health care costs and indirect costs such as lost worker productivity.

While the article referred to the population in general, not just Latinos, I found it fascinating and alarming that Latinos run twice the risk for developing Type 2 diabetes as people in the mainstream. The Latino community in the United States is growing by leaps and bounds, but our health risks are also. We need to do something about it. Some cases of diabetes result from genetic, or hereditary, causes, but the majority of cases result from poor eating habits, lack of exercise, and being overweight. You can find more information by calling your doctor or by contacting the American Diabetes Association. You can also find information on the Internet. The point is, we must begin to take care of ourselves and our children, and we must start immediately.

As a case in point, some months ago, I took my son to see his first live "Barney" show. He was thrilled about seeing his hero, and I was delighted for him. As we sat in the audience, though, I saw something that gave me pause. I was somewhat taken aback and saddened by the condition of the families who surrounded us. One family sitting behind us was Latino, and in true fashion, included all the immediate family: the kids, the parents, and Grandpa and Grandma. There were at least ten of them. What really got my attention was that the kids, who were between five and seven years of age, were all grossly overweight. At nine o'clock at night, these kids were stuffing themselves with popcorn, sodas, and huge piles of cotton candy.

My son kept asking me if he could have what those kids were eating, but I refused to give in. He was allowed one treat, and that was that. We as parents must be able to control what our children eat so that we can keep them fit and healthy. It's a lifelong habit, and starts at a very young age. What chance do kids have if they start out 20 to 30 pounds heavier than they should be? It doesn't only affect their bodies; it affects their self-esteem as well when other kids laugh at them. Who will they turn to when Mom and Dad are not there to comfort them with potato chips and candy?

What Can We Do About It?

I asked a dear friend of mine, Norma Molina, who is a registered dietitian (RD) and a certified lactation educator (CLE), with a certificate in adult weight management, that very question. Norma conducts nutrition education classes and workshops for children, parents, and business professionals in both English and Spanish. She specializes in infant, child, and family nutrition, weight loss management, and nutrition as a specialty. She also provides nutrition consultation services and medical nutrition therapy. Norma has been interviewed on both radio and TV stations as a nutrition expert on many occasions. Our conversation was so interesting, I decided to formally interview her so that I could share her knowledge with my readers.

Daniel: In this "hurry here, hurry there" world we live in, how can we eat in a healthy way when we are eating at fast food restaurants almost every day?

Norma: It is true that we live in a fast-paced world. But making small steps toward good health *can* be done.

For example, if you are going to eat at a fast food restaurant, look for the most nutritious item on the menu. Pick grilled items rather than fried ones. Ask them to hold the mayonnaise, and ask for extra lettuce and tomatoes. To give the sandwich flavor, I usually ask for a package of barbeque sauce. That cuts down on the fat.

Daniel: What about exercise? What can we do to make an effort to improve our health?

Norma: All it takes to be in an active mode is for adults to exercise 30 minutes every day. It doesn't even have to be all at one time—it can be spread out over the day. For example, instead of parking your car close to your office, try parking farther and walking. Take the stairs instead of taking the elevator. Kids, on the other hand, need at least 60 minutes of hard exercise or activity daily.

Daniel: What about snacks? Are there snacks we can eat that can help us in our effort to be healthier? I have heard of people freezing fruits and vegetables to have healthier treats, for example.

Norma: Yes! As a matter of fact, one of the most popular frozen fruits are grapes. You can buy low-fat ice cream and put the grapes on top of it for a tasty treat. Fresh smoothies are snacks that everyone loves. I also recommend low-fat string cheese. Kids especially enjoy that. I have many patients who eat celery sticks and apple slices with natural peanut butter. Any kind of fresh fruit is wonderful. The key for kids is to make it fun by cutting the fruit up in funny shapes, which also makes the fruit easier to consume.

Walnuts and almonds are great treats that also have the omega-3 fatty acids we all need. They're good for both kids and adults. An old-fashioned peanut butter sandwich on healthy bread will please any kid!

Daniel: How do we go about getting our daily allowance of fruits and vegetables? Do we make it harder than it really is?

Norma: It's a lot easier to get your fruits and vegetables than you think. It only takes half a cup of cooked vegetables, or one cup of raw vegetables to make a serving. We need five servings of fruits and vegetables a day! We can get our daily requirements sometimes simply by eating a salad at lunch.

Daniel: So it's really not five whole fruits and five whole vegetables a day? Wow! I feel better already!

Norma: If people take the time to calculate the number of true servings of fruits and vegetables they get in one day, they will be surprised! They are probably getting pretty close!

Daniel: What about our Latino diet can we change to make for a healthier meal?

Norma: The good news is that there are very good things about our diet. We use a lot of vegetables in our dishes, and we eat corn tortillas, which are a great source of nutrition.

Daniel: So what are the challenges in our traditional diet?

Norma: The thing that I see is that we use a lot of cheese and cream in our foods. These things add a lot of empty calories to our foods. We also have a tendency to fry many of our foods, which is not a healthy way to prepare meals.

Daniel: What can we do?

Norma: If you're going to use cheese, shred it, or buy it shredded. When you put shredded cheese on your plate, it looks like a lot. But if you slice it, it takes a lot more cheese to make it look equal. With cream, use low-fat sour cream. I'll admit that I've been told that this changes the flavor of the dish, so I compromise by recommending people use half cream and half low-fat cheese. Any attempt is better than nothing. We can also use our salsas instead of cream to give our food flavor.

Daniel: How do we get around the frying?

Norma: Instead of frying, try baking foods. We can also use small portions of olive oil and canola oil to cook our foods. We can use nonstick cooking sprays so we still get the fried flavor, but the food isn't swimming or saturated in oil.

Daniel: Any other advice?

Norma: Yes. We are the role models for our children. We start learning our relationship to foods at a very young age. The key is to teach your child how to eat healthy right from the get-go, and you must be the role model in teaching them, not by words alone, but by *showing* them how to do it. I would also encourage you to eat more at home instead of eating out. The danger of eating out every day is that our children will grow up not knowing how to cook, and they will resort to eating fast foods or unhealthy microwave dishes. Make small changes in your diet, and over a period of time you will begin to head toward a healthier diet.

Daniel: Can you give us a couple of recipes for healthy snacks?

Norma: We can cut out fat calories in lots of our meals and dishes without having to sacrifice mouth-watering flavors. Fruits and vegetables make great ingredients in recipes and provide body-healthy antioxidants like beta-carotene and vitamin C, and body-healthy fiber, too. Instead of adding creamy sauces, gravies, Mexican creams, and mayo-based dressings, try colorful, fresh, and zesty salsas as toppings. Salsas are no longer just your traditional tomato-and-chili-ingredient salsas. There are so many different varieties that include an assortment of vegetables, herbs, spices, and even fruits. You can find cookbooks that focus on just salsas alone! Have fun and create some of your own salsas that are full of flavor, color, and texture. Then try them with grilled chicken, fish, or beef dishes, on crackers, with cheeses, in burritos, pita bread, tacos, tostadas, salads, and of course, with baked or low-fat chips. Salsas also make great appetizer and sandwich accompaniments.

Here's a unique salsa recipe that you can try with your next grilled meal or burrito.

Mango-Strawberry Salsa

2 large ripe mangos, peeled, seeded, and chopped
2 cups of fresh strawberries, washed and chopped
1/2 to 1 small chili pepper, seeded and finely
    chopped (or if you don't like *hot*, use 1 green bell
    pepper seeded and finely chopped)
1/4 cup of finely chopped red onion
1/4 cup finely chopped fresh mint leaves
2 tablespoons lime juice
2 tablespoons honey

Mix all of the ingredients together in a bowl, then chill in the refrigerator for two or more hours to blend all of the great flavors together. Serve and enjoy!

Children love smoothies! You can serve them for breakfast, snacks, or desserts. Smoothies are high in calcium and low in calories if made with low-fat dairy products and/or calcium-enriched orange juice. Use fresh fruits or frozen fruits as ingredients to increase your child's daily intake of fruit, vitamin C, and fiber.

Here is a scrumptious smoothie recipe your children will love!

Berry Banana Smoothie

1 banana cut into small slices
1 cup chopped berries, like strawberries, blueberries,
    raspberries, and/or blackberries, fresh or frozen
1/2 cup 2%, 1%, or nonfat milk
1 cup low-fat vanilla yogurt (or frozen yogurt)
1/2 cup calcium-enriched orange juice (frozen juice
    can be used instead)

Place all ingredients in a blender and cover tightly. Blend well for about a minute. If too thick, add a couple of ice cubes until smoothly blended. Makes two or three tall glass servings.

For more nutrition information, you can e-mail Norma at norma@normasnutritioninfo.com.

Index

The Dream Planner
Journaling From Greatness

With Guided Meditation CD

Daniel Gutierrez

Dreaming is our human right. All of us are designed for greatness and have the ability to dream. When we are children, we dream big. We dream of great families, cars, relationships and wealth. Unfortunately, the world begins to tell us that we can't have what we desire, and one day we wake up and realize that we believe that too.

Life sometimes wears us down and our dreams become just some place we go to get away from reality, not really understanding or believing that if we can dream it, we can have it.

The Dream Planner is designed for you to get back to what is important in life. Dreaming and believing that anything we desire is possible is the first step. Take *The Dream Planner* seriously and write only those dreams you truly desire. Carry your planner everywhere you go, and when doubt or fear sets in, look back to your planner, listen to that voice inside of you that says "yes" and take action immediately. The results will amaze you.

Daniel has included twelve of his favorite photos and poems to guide you along the way to achieving your dreams.

Dream BIG and accept your greatness.